GOLDEN
PURPOSES
OF LIFE

WAYNE LINDSEY

Matador
9 Priory Business Park,
Wistow Road, Kibworth Beauchamp,
Leicestershire. LE8 0RX
Tel: 0116 279 2299
Email: books@troubador.co.uk
Web: www.troubador.co.uk/matador
Twitter: @matadorbooks

ISBN 978 183859 265 3

British Library Cataloguing in Publication Data.
A catalogue record for this book is available from the British Library.

Printed and bound in Great Britain by 4edge Limited
Typeset in 12pt Ten Oldstyle by Troubador Publishing Ltd, Leicester, UK

Matador is an imprint of Troubador Publishing Ltd

CONTENTS

AUTHOR'S PERSONAL MOTTOS

Happiness is the birthright of every human being.
(Wayne Lindsey)

All human beings are born with the natural,
incredible ability to realize and strive to achieve
their true potential.
(Wayne Lindsey)

Every human being should feel appreciated, may we
all be awaken to this.
(Wayne Lindsey)

Be clear about your goals that can bring you
happiness, stay committed and focus on them.
(Wayne Lindsey)

Be driven, determined and dedicated to find success
and a healthy well-being.
(Wayne Lindsey)

Be ambitious, but don't belittle others once you
achieved success.
(Wayne Lindsey)

AUTHOR'S THREE WISHES

1. Wishing all readers of this book peace and love.
2. Wishing all readers of this book a happy and improved quality of life.
3. Wishing all readers of this book good health, all the joy and success, you ever asked for.

ACKNOWLEDGEMENTS

I am indebted to a network of precious friends who illuminate my life with. Happiness, love, their creative thinking, constructive criticism, inspiration and other magnificent contributions to my journey in writing this book, namely ; Dave, Julia, Kelly, Hayley and Ryan.

I feel privileged by the wisdom and support shown by two wise ladies. Rosalind Moody, Joy Palmer and a wise man Nick Cooke who has over 30 years as a clinical practitioner and over 17 years has a trainer, who shares my passion for self-development.

With the help of all these wonderful people, *Golden purposes of Life* will continue to shine a light on a brighter future.

To you all My grateful thanks.

W L

INTRODUCTION

We live in a frantic world, people are rushing to and fro; There is so much pressure today on both young and old. There are homelessness, marriages and relationships failures everywhere. Suicides, drug addiction and alcoholics at an all time high.

Some people say they live for their families, their own flesh and blood. On other occasion people say. "Thread on who you can, get what you want no matter what the consequences get rich quick". Others say life's only about survival.

Surely life is deeper than this. Which is why so many people ask these questions.

o   What is the purpose of life?
o   How can I be happy?
o   What hope is there for me?
o   How important can finding life's purpose be?
o   Does it matter what I believe?
o   Will we ever enjoy real happiness?
o   What does the future hold?
o   What are the worst problem facing mankind today?

POEM 1:
WHAT IS LIFE?

What is life? No one seems they can truly tell.

They asked me the same question again. What is life?
Perhaps it's just a spell.

We search for reasons, and also meanings, but really
it's who we spend our time with, the things we do,
and the things we believe in.

Some people have lots of sorrows, others have lots
of joys.

It would be wonderful to bless our eyes each morning,
as we must face each day, come what may.

As we mix with friends and foes, sometimes the ups
and down of life can take us through some serious
phase.

Never give up no matter how your feeling stressing.

Live your life has if it's a good blessing.

Strive to be happy and make the best of the world
we're all born into.

Wayne Lindsey

POEM 2:
A WONDERFUL WORLD

Every now and then we all need to stop for a minute
to just appreciate the beauty that surround us. The
things we take for granted because we see it every day.
The fresh cut grass, the beautiful flowers, the warm
summer breeze blowing through our hair, the colors
of the rainbow, innocence of a young mind, it's full
of majesty and wonder, everything in it's elegant
charmed and refine beauty.
Sometimes ignorance and pain makes us leave this
all behind, imaging never seeing the stars on a clear
night sky.
Instead of fussing, fighting, and backbiting we could
come together and enjoy a wonderful world.
Before we know it. It will be too late so let's make
good, positive use of it, and don't hesitate.

Wayne Lindsey

POEM 3:
IT'S YOUR WORLD AND MINE

Imagine living in a world where there is no war?
There would be a brighter and more hopeful future
for the human race.
Children could grow up in harmony to take our place,
we can have peace and love which we should all
embrace.
Visualize you're on a beautiful beach with your loved
one walking on the golden sand, holding hands.
As the sunset start to fall people with lovely smiles on
their faces watching it all.
Imagine if we had more integrity, and more unity,
this world would be filled with more tranquility.
All these things should not be a person's fantasy it
can become our reality, if we all agree that it's your
world and mine.

Wayne Lindsey

SCENARIOS

SCENARIO

It was a cool and lovely Sunday afternoon. A heavy flurry of overnight rain had encouraged plants to flower, the dust on the ground came alive, the bloom of flowers and fruits vied for a spot with nature's beauty, birds where singing merely, even foxes who normally comes out when it's dark came out of their lair to enjoy the delights of spring.

Dave and I were heading to a friend's wedding anniversary party. Listening to the radio, an advert for gift aid support came on which lead to this conversation between Dave and I.

Dave: {Sighing heavily} Man oh man! What is life? What is the true purpose of life? Why is this world such an unfair place to live in.

Myself: There's nothing wrong with this world it's human nature that make the world feel unfair sometimes.

Dave: I don't get it. It was only a few months ago I was having a debate on why we have so much challenges and suffering in our lives. I've been questioning the direction of my life recently, wishing I could have less complications.

Myself: It sounds like you're having a crisis. And I understand how difficult this situation is for you. Have you ever thought about things that could help you look at your current situation differently such as acceptance and commitment therapy or pastoral counseling —

Dave: {interrupt} I don't want to talk about any pastor or no father above, as I see people praying and all he seems to do is stare at them.

Myself: That is ok if you don't want to. I get the feeling you are wanting things to change more significantly to reach your self ideal. However ACT therapy, and pastoral counseling, could be a useful tool to help you.

Dave: {Picking away at his tooth with the same finger which went up his nose several times} I'm not interesting in any counseling.

I actively listened to Dave, to get a clear and accurate understanding of his views. I wanted to motivate Dave so I wrote him two poems entitled, What is life? And it's your world and mine. This is to help Dave visualize the kind of happy existence he would hope for.

After reading the poems, Dave was happy.

LOOK AT LIFE

LOOK AT LIFE

Sooner or later, a lot of people wonder what the purpose of life is. Is it to work hard to improve the quality of our living conditions? Some people can't face up to life with all it's pressure they are always looking for a way out. Many people in life feel that the main purpose in living is to acquire material wealth. They believe that this can lead to a happy meaningful life. Yet the statistics show that a baffling number of wealthy people are not happy.

Some people doubt that life has any purpose when they experience long suffering and challenges. I've heard many people asking these questions.

o Will my suffering ever end?
o What is the purpose of life?
o What marvelous outlook do I have for the future?
o How can I be happy?
o Does it matter what I believe?
o Will we ever enjoy real happiness?
o What does the future hold?
o How important is can finding life's purpose be?

Humans are born with free will, that is, with the ability to choose. We are not made like robots who are guided mainly by instinct. So humans can choose what they believe in.

Everyone wants to be happy and live a meaningful life. But many problems threaten our pursuit for happiness. The current state of human society is in many ways contrary to our natural desire for a peaceful, secure and happy life.

Mother Teresa had this to say about life;

> *"Life is an opportunity, benefit from it. Life is beauty, admire it. Life is a dream, realize it. Life is a challenge, meet it. Life is a duty, complete it. Life is a game, play it. Life is a promise, fulfill it. Life is sorrow, overcome it. Life is a song, sing it. Life is a struggle, accept it. Life is a tragedy, confront it. Life is an adventure, dare it. Life is luck, make it. Life is too precious, do not destroy it. Life is life, fight for it."*

I don't like breaking things, people hearts, and promises. I promise some friends and associates, that I would do my best to answer their questions about life purposes, as much as I can.

MEANINGLESS OR MEANINGFUL

The meaning of life expresses itself in the living of life, not in a set of words about the living of life.

It only takes a little observation to realize that life is a process of change and growth, adaptation and renewal, healing and learning, creativity and transformation. When the process of life is expressing itself freely the subjective experience is one of physical, emotional, mental, and/or spiritual pleasure in varying degrees. If you strongly resist any part of the process of life, you will experience varying degrees of physical, emotional, and mental, pain.

A lot of people ask about the meaning of life, they are really asking "What is the purpose of life?" And underneath or behind that question is "How can I make my life more meaningful (i.e., important, purposeful, or worthwhile)?"

Life is so phenomenal intricate that we will not fully understand life entirely. The greatest aspect about life, is that no human can put a truthful meaning to it. The main purpose of life is to strive to live totally with contentment and happiness through experiences and explorations. You don't need anyone's permission and you don't have to live according to someone else's idea of a meaningful life, but sometimes other people do have good suggestions.

What seems to bring about people to complain that life lacks any purpose or meaning are various experiences of unhappiness. Such as poor relationship, illnesses, poverty, poor communication.

We can have meaningful lives. It's important to affirm that a purposeful, rich, happy, and meaningful life is within the bounds of our possibility.

CURIOSITY

Curiosity is the state of genuinely wanting to know more about the world and people around us. It creates an openness to unfamiliar activities and lays the ground work to create greater opportunities to experience self-discovery.

Curiosity can be nurtured and developed through practice and using its tremendous powers to turn everyday experiences to ones that are intriguing, wondrous, educational, and successful.

It all starts with wanting to know more about the world around us. Curiosity at its core is about noticing and been drawn to things we find interesting it's also about seizing the pleasures in life. When we are curios we see things differently, we use our powers of observation more fully, we feel alive and engaged more, we become more capable of embracing opportunities, making connections and experiencing moments of insights and meaning, all of which provide a foundation for a rich awareness and satisfying life experience.

A lot of people in this world still struggle to figure out; what they are meant to do, what excites them?

And what brings out the best in them? This is where curiosity can be fundamental to our success. Figuring things out will help you discover amazing things about your own life, and what you can do now and in the future.

You may not have a clear vision for your own purpose in life yet, but probably curious about things. Those interesting things that happens to your unique motivation and what drives you. Pursuing them will set you on the path of unlocking who you are.

If we are going to find meaning or purpose in life, the chances are it will come from our natural curiosity. For example, our hobbies, passions, and our interest. Curiosity very clearly is the stepping stone to inventions, creativity, motivations, hope, and personal happiness.

HUMAN'S SUFFERING

There is so much going on in the world, things and times seems so critical. Yet I don't want you to worry your minds or for you to give up on your ambitions, roles or visions, goals or missions. More and more illnesses are discovered each year, problematic or maladaptive behaviors are increasing, complaints of pain and sorrows are at an all time high.

What are the causes of suffering? If suffering were created by mother nature, there would be no way to overcome it. We are the one's making suffering out of ourselves, its our choice. All humans got a choice, instead of creating more joy, peace, happiness, blissfulness, being ecstatic for ourselves and others, we tend to create more misery for ourselves.

Take a good look at the world and the people in it, vast amount of human beings are suffering in all aspects of life. For example, we suffer from loneliness, poverty, war or crime, disasters. We suffer not only psychically, but also mentally and emotionally as well.

These things in life are not hard to endure. Pain is part of life, some are short, others are long. Acute pain is intense but short. Chronic pain most times is long but dull.

Whenever we see loved ones suffers, it grieves us, we suffer our own anguish at their pain. We need to action by creating pleasure for others, all human beings are born with the necessary capability and intelligence to make comfort for others and ourselves. Which means we can transcend out of our intelligence. To accomplish this we require education and right actions clearer understanding and better communication. In general in the world, people seek an education not for the sake of future lives but to to reduce pain and increase pleasure in our lives and others.

An earthquake, a hurricane, or a volcano destroys a small island. Cancer takes a single father life leaving behind two innocent children. A teenager is knife by another teenager by mistaken identity.

When tragedies or disasters like these happen. Many of us ask why this world is full of suffering and hatred. It is easy to see why. Humans like to afflict their emotions on to other humans, they want to be more important and powerful than others. So they go to war, fight and bully others.

Sometimes people suffer because of unexpected events when they are in the wrong place at the wrong time bad things or accidents can happen to them.

Humans have tried in vain with every kind of rulers or government for centuries without success.

Yes, they have made advances with technologies. However, there is still a lot of poverty, crimes, injustice, and war.

This could become a little bit easier, if each humans were allowed the right to use there free will (freedom of choice) about whom we want to be and the positive things we want to do with our lives, also by helping each other day by day.

Another ease in suffering comes by accepting and appreciating just how little we need to flourish, and how abundant nature seems to be in supplying our needs. We can only vary our pleasures to a certain limit and ease our pain.

We may also suffer because of choices from others. Humans have been afflicting the most disturbing evils from time. From burning other humans alive to abusing young children. We refuse to use our free will for peace, so instead we misuse it by bringing suffering onto others.

Imagine living in a world where there is no war. Just visualized it, waking up each day without having to worry about oppression, economic uncertainty, discrimination. Does this sound too good to be true?

PEACE AND SECURITY

Whenever we face complex challenges in our lives, we trend to feel that inner peace and security are elusive. Do you truly believe that we can solve all the many challenges that we face along life journey? Remember behavior usually reflects our thoughts, feelings, beliefs,desires and our environment.

Humans has been unable to find a cure for the evil traits that lurk within us.

I honesty believe that we are unable to make the world safe and secure for all living organism on earth. We simple haven't got the limitations to do so. All humans has the universal responsibility to share compassion and kindness the solid rock that we need to bring forth more peace and security in our societies.

We can try to remember that natural calamities such as flooding should be accepted as these things are out of our control. All living creatures both great and small seek peace and security. Life is precious to these creatures as it his to all human beings. We all strive for protection from dangers that threatened our lives.

A collaboration and resilient relationship within all human's across societies is a fundamental element of peace and security. Functional relationships allows us to understand the needs and interest of others, and hence place a platform for empathy, knowledge and wisdom to make useful actions.

We all know that people are the same in every continent on planet earth, their is good and bad in everyone. However, we can try to live with each other in peace and harmony.It was ordained for human beings to live in peace and unity. Peace, love and security is the beauty of the world. So let it start shining within us.

INTEGRITY

Integrity is the key to a good life. Because obviously, if we violate our own hearts, if we go against our own conscience, we cannot live freely, happily, openly, with others. It's when we obey the law of love and rightness written in our hearts that we feel connected to all, and full of life.

Destiny and well-being depend on integrity. Our confidence, our openness to love and intimacy, our ability to stay close to others, all come and go according to how well we follow our hearts.

In integrity we live without it we die. Being untrue to your heart can destroy your life, and create your own personal miseries. Each moment in life, each choice is a fork in the road. Which way will we go? Where will we end up? It depends on how well we obey our hearts.

When we violate our own feelings about what's right and what we should be doing, we shut down and turn away from happiness, love, and all the most beautiful things in life, we just don't think beauty fits us well, so we reject it. But when we follow our hearts and our conscience, we open up to life, and let it flood in. Of course not all negative actions are equally consequential, and neither are all positive actions. How strongly an action or choice affects your destiny depends on how important it is to you. If it is crucial to your heart, then it is crucial. No matter if it seems trivial to others, no matter if it would be called unimportant by religion or culture.

If a person sincerely believes they should become more disciplined, they will feel terrible if they don't . It will hangover their head like a dark cloud, changing the tone of their life for the worse, even if nobody else cares about it. For that individual there is no greater condemnation than that which they would visit upon themselves for having betrayed their own heart.

That shows exactly how personal this really is. It makes no difference what anyone else says; a person is condemned by their own hand.

The heart recognizes that no matter what we do, we are good, and we are capable of doing good. When we see that we have done wrong, the heart would jump to correct it, and to heal it;

Rather than step in shame and self-hatred.

We don't need to condemn ourselves. But it is good that we condemn our wrong actions, and that we reject badness. That is our divine sensitivity at work. So, this is not clarion call to throw away the power of discernment; our actions do not change the person we essentially are. They do not rid us of the basic goodness and sensitivity place in our hearts.

People who are following their heart want to peace, love, commitment, loyalty, reliability, all values that the human heart values highly.

Remember: Life is also an integrity test.

WHAT DO YOU WANT?

The bold sovereign never ceases to make life determining declarations. Granted some of them may seem a bit perverse, but even when they are, we will still get what we want. There's no accounting for waste, is there?

Someone may be creating misery, but even then, he's winning, that's what he wants. Perhaps a man doesn't think that beautifully surrendered and cooperative would be a success, or that being disciplined would be a victory. He feels that these things would be loss. And you see, he wants to win in the terms he presently values most of us feel the same way, we want to win. So you win always. There's no question about that. The only question is, what your victory will be. To what outcome do you apply your mind? What do you want? What is your purpose right now? Not just in theory , but in practice. For example everyone wants love, both in theory and in the depths of their soul. Even so, in practice a lot of energy goes into fearing love, and even sabotaging it and you will create according to the dominant goals of your mind and heart.

Maybe we're winning, but what about the fact that our "victories" can be bittersweet; they all have downsides, side effects that create pain and problems for ourselves and others. Naturally, that raises a question; Why in the world would I do something that has downsides?

Well, why would you take the train everywhere, given the downside of the cost of train tickets? The fact is, we make thousands of choices despite their downsides, and generally in full awareness of them.

The bottom line? Life is full of trade offs. There isn't one single move on the chessboard that doesn't have upsides and downsides. So you may as well make your choice and accept the inevitable costs of that choice, because you cannot have the upsides of your choice without it's downsides. There's no point whinging unless you want to.

If you wish, look at each downside you're complaining about, or suffering from. See why it is indeed a downside of a choice you made. See why each particular downside inevitable, based on your choices.

You make your bed and you lie in it. But what if, at some point, you'd like a different set of upsides and downsides than the set you're looking at right now? Then you can change your choice anytime you like, you can look at your choice, look at your results, decide to change your position.

If you look at your years of experience and consider what happened, you will now be able to better understand why things happened as they did; consciously or otherwise, you put considerable energy into creating the way things happened. And you will understand why even what you considered to be a defeat was in fact a victory. That's good to know. Now you can be conscious of processes that may have been unconscious before.

Failure is not a threat for one who always wins. Therefore, have no fear of failure. It never has happened, and never will! Nor are you under pressure to succeed, since success is a given. This brings a very new and interesting meaning to the expression "failure is not an option".

I don't want people to feel they have to choose on thing over another. Just see the results you're getting and decide if you like them. Also appreciate the ways in which you participated in the creation of those results.

FAITH

Faith is the power of our convictions and expectations. Like the wind we can't see faith, but we can feel it, and see its effects on our lives and, just as the direction and speed of the wind determines the weather, the nature of our faith shapes our destiny.

Having positive faith is the essential ingredient for a beautiful life. But faith alone will not do the trick. We also need to bring effort born from our faith.

WHAT FAITH PREVENTS OR ALLOWS

Here's one way way our faith shapes our destiny; out of all that might be possible and desirable for us, we only pursue what we believe in. Negative or insufficient faith prevents good things, because no sane person would invest effort trying to do something considered to be impossible. And, even if we think it's doable, we won't do something we feel is foolish or otherwise dangerous. For example, a woman won't get married if she believes she's just going to get hurt. Positive faith is a go button and negative faith is a no go.

Every person who ever worked for a dream had the confidence that if they did so, they would succeed. Lacking such confidence, we won't try for our goal, we'll load our attempt with so much doubt that we'll sabotage our efforts. As you know, a man who believes he is unworthy of the woman he loves will either fail to pursue her, or he will pursue her in an insecure, half-hearted spirit, practically ensuring rejection. He would need much more positive faith if he wants to win her love.

We often approach our goals with an attitude of unfaith and hopelessness, pulling our punches, cutting corners, and then getting disappointing results. Of course, we're not surprised when that happens after all, isn't that what we expected?

WHAT FAITH ALONE CAN'T DO

Positive faith is only part of what it takes to create a beautiful life. Once you believe that good things are possible for you. You still have to go forth armed with your positive convictions, and do what it takes to create a beauty and goodness in your life. For example, we all know than an athlete needs faith to win the Olympics; but it's silly to believe that anyone could win the Olympics due to faith alone. To win the gold also requires discipline, regular training, a good diet, sufficient rest, an excellent coach. Faith opens the door to every kind of success, but we still have to pick up our feet and walk through. True faith is not blind faith. It would be insane, not faithful, to believe that something good will happen we're not fulfilling the preconditions for that thing to happen. Positive faith is the first precondition for success are found not just on effort, or even smart effort, but also in character and attitude. People ask, "Does marriage work?" Presumably, that is a general philosophical question. But, you see, a useful answer can't be generalized. The realistic answer is do what it takes for the marriage to work. If you are loving, ego-transcending, caring, loyal, forgiving, and compassionate, then most likely marriage will work for you. But what if you are intolerant, impatient, and selfish? Then, of course it won't work.

The odds of success in any given endeavor are not the same for everyone, it depends on how well each aspirant fulfills the preconditions. All things are, in that sense, conditional. And therefore, all reasonable faith is conditional not non-conditional.

So then, does faith work? Yes, if it is reasonable when you are willing to fulfill the requirements for what yo desire, then you have every reason to have faith, and your faith will work.

Give yourself a decent chance. Otherwise, the only faith that is justified for you is faith that things won't work. Life can't work if you don't work, and it can't work right if you don't work right.

Great ideas, great goals and great intentions are meaningless without great actions. People achieve success in life not just because they take charge of their thoughts and beliefs, but because their thoughts and beliefs propels them into taking action.

LOVE

Love is the honest attempt to make you and others happy. It's being sincerely, happily, unselfishly oriented to our needs, our welfare, our furtherance. Love is not about doing things that work to our own personal advantage. Love is something that we do for the benefit of others; we feel happiest when we're loving; we feel more ourselves.

Love begins where, small ego-driven, self-interest ends. And love ends when self-interest takes over. Love can be sweet, wonderful and juicy other times it can be the pearl of a great price, as well as it should be.

Love tunes us up. In the process, it awakens psychic awareness, raises consciousness, and enlivens the body/mind. People who are sincerely in love feel some remarkable things, things that are out of this world. They experience a strong mind-heart, genuine connections to their love ones. They not only feel happy, the look happy and radiant. They see the world as bright and wonderful place.

It is far more theory, a philosophic position. Love is passion, beauty, desire, a true healing power, the spring of heartfelt kindness. Passion love are so bounteous that they fill the heart with overflowing. And that overflow is a gape. You fill up your heart, and then you fill up the world.

When you share love, you find yourself loving everything. You experience your affinity with all of life.We all love in a personal fashion. No heart wants to love universally only. We want to love personally too.

Yes, love will make you happy. Yes, love does you good. But even so, remember: Getting something for yourself is not the purpose for loving. Always love is for helping and healing.

WHY IS TRUE LOVE SO CHALLENGING?

True love is indeed a straight and narrow path. To walk that path successfully you must avoid aberrances and dangers that lie on both sides of it. One must avoid the inherent dangers of personal attachment and re-activity that can make human to human love less than loving. And must try to overcome the inadequacy agape, which is the impersonal or depersonalized love can be less convincing, acceptable, and effective in the human context.

True love heals the short comings of the agape approach, which fails to deeply satisfy human loved one's because it lacks true recognition and appreciation of individual personality, true human affinity, true bonding and loyalty, and true personal investment or vulnerability. True love will always recognizes and embraces the uniqueness of each human being that it meets and exceeds the requirements of the human heart on any levels.

POWER OF LOVE

There is no greater power in the Universe than the power of love. An army of beautiful butterflies dancing in your stomach, getting week at the knees, stars in your eyes, looking and feeling as happy as the Chesire Cat in Alice's adventures in wonderland. Giving and receiving true love which never dies is a feeling like no other. For me, the feeling of love is the highest frequency you can emit.

Love is a condition of our minds brought about by consistent performance, and serenity of our souls. Love is what makes the journey in our lives worthwhile.

When we are in love we do all sorts of things to get a response from our love ones. The bonds and conditions we have with other people, stands to give us a greater sense of meaning of well-being and purpose, loves helps to determine the quality of our relationships, which determine the quality of our lives.

Love is a fundamental need for human's, stability, security, adventures, connections, belonging, freedom and positive energy.

Human's need a legacy of deserving love. Without a decent amount of love in our early years, we will feel normal to be disliked. However learning to love yourself can heal you, it allows you to take on new positive perspectives an eradicate negative thoughts from our minds.

Love can hep us to select and connect with joy and nourishment, satisfaction and affections, energy and protection. One of the best way to love things and others is to simultaneously, unconditionally love yourself.

To unconditionally love and accept yourself takes commitment and discipline but it will give you a gratifying feeling of living a happy life. And grow stronger with sharing love to others.

GOOD RAPPORT

You've heard the admonition, "Know thyself". To know yourself deeply and accept yourself accurately puts you in touch with the various parts of human nature. Then you also recognize those deeper springs of humanity in others.

To have good rapport with others, we need to access to parts of humanity that, presently we may not quite want to be, think we should be, or even like to believe that we are. When we open those doors in ourselves, we can open those doors in others.

Facing your own personal patterns can help greatly with rapport. When you see another person manifesting some pattern you have faced in yourself, you can easily understand it. If, for example, you've ever been defensive, or stubborn, and you see someone doing that same thing, you can understand what they are feeling, identify with them, and have compassion for them. And if they're open to it, you might even be able to help them deal with those difficult feelings, all from your experience from handling them in yourself.

Whether we want to admit it or not, each of us has considerable understanding of our own neuroses, social mistakes, and the like. Often ironically,we tend to be less willing to acknowledge and understand many essentially positive things we have in common with other people. Taboos come and go in cycles, and the "soft", and feeling parts of human nature are the current "taboos", things that people fear in themselves. For examples, our own healthy needs for love, for understanding, for life. Our sensitivity, passion, vulnerability, dependence, caring. The troubles, those things are the basic common ground of positive human qualities and needs. If we fear those things, we may find it nearly impossible to bridge to others.

Every human being is qualified to understand other human beings. As human's we all have a lot in common. Any human can honestly say. I know how human beings feel, because I am a human being." And that fact gives every human being the perfect resource for rapport building: empathy. For example, imagine someone feels invalidated. Well, we all know a lot about feeling invalidated. And what if they are ignored? We know that feeling too. We're specialists on what it feels like to be ignored! In fact, we're specialist on just about every human feeling in the book, because we've had them all.

We've been left out, included, critized, invalidated, and, bored, and everything else. We even recognize various flavors of each feeling. For example, wrongly complimented, correctly complimented, ingratiatingly complimented, manipulatively complimented we know them all. We know the many shades of happy, the many shades of sad.

Although human responses vary, responses follow familiar patterns, so much that most people can easily put the shoe on the other foot and walk a mile in the other person moccasins if they want to. But it's amazing how many how many people fail to apply what they know about their own human emotions to others. Empathy can actively allow you to do so, it is a core cornerstone to effective rapport.

Good rapport allows you to:

o To be competent to address more life issues that a person present within your conversations.
o Encourages the person to speak freely about his/ her experiences.
o Helps you to interpret the person's thoughts, feelings and behaviors.
o Helps you develop the person trust.
o Helps you navigate the person's journey.

Life can become quite interesting when you look at things from a new angle. Lets take a look at it from the George Theory Angle.

THE GEORGE CARLIN THEORY

The most unfair thing about life is the way it ends – I mean, life is tough. It takes up a lot of your time and what do you get at the end of it? Death. I mean, what's that , a bonus? I think the life cycle is all backwards. You should die first get it out of the way. Then you move to an old peoples home. You get kicked out when you're too young, you get a gold watch and then you go to work. You work for forty years until you're young enough to enjoy your retirement. You have fun, party plenty, then you get ready for senior school. Then you go to junior school, you become a kid, you play and you have no responsibilities. You become a little baby, you go back into the womb, spend your last nine months, floating, and you finish off as an orgasm.

The ability to succeed in life is in inextricably link to our ability to deal with people. To know how best to deal with others, we need to start trying to understand them. When we appreciate how and why people view the world differently and respond appropriately to that, we are able to connect and engage with them at a completely new level.

CRITICAL THINKING

Critical thinking is the careful application of reason in the determination of whether a claim is true. (More and Parker)

"A judicious reasoning about what to believe and, therefore, what to do." (Tittle)

Critical thinking requires:

a) Careful, intentional thinking

b) Use of reason or logic

c) Judgments about beliefs

d) Application to real world problems

Critical thinking is not fast or easy process to think critically, you have to focus on the issues at hand taking in all it's complexities.

The goal of critical thinking is not to decide whether to accept or reject an argument. In critical thinking the goal is to fully evaluate all parts of a claim, that someone has made to assess each of its parts as well as the whole. Critical thinking allows you to determine whether you agree or disagree. It allows you to explain why you disagree or agree to an argument.

Critical thinking is an exercise in collective problem solving. Critical thinking is also important for your understanding and thought processes.

When we are asked to think critically. We are asked to take a position regarding the truth or acceptability of something.

We live in a frantic world, which people hold widely different views on many topics. Individuals, communities, businesses need to make decisions on many issues, that are the subject of strong disagreements.

Critical thinking helps us offer reasons' action and evaluate reasons of others. It is active, not passive. It helps solves problems effectively, discover truths, clearly communicate, and helps us live a flourishing life.

HUMANITY

Many of us are diligently searching, on various levels, for solutions to humanity's personal, interpersonal, and global problems. Many of us fervently strive for spiritual growth and fulfillment. Few suspects what a rich but unused resource for both we have at our fingertips, and in our hearts, our own humanity.

The primary cause of humanity's problems is not greed, or insensitivity, or dogmatism. It's that we don't understand who we are. And consequently, we don't live as who we are. When we cut corners on being human, economizing has its price. All over the world, even in our personal lives, we witness the heavy cost of hesitating to be fully, truly human – to love deeply, to serve unstintingly, to live passionately, to openly depend on others, to live our positive desires. When will we recognize this reluctance as the true cause of our suffering, and correct it?

Our individual well-being and the collective destiny of ourselves depend on the living expression of all, of our truly human characteristics. Until and unless human nature is resurrected from the trash bin in its entire and real goodness, we cannot be optimally effective in:

o Relating positively to ourselves
o Relating effectively to others
o Relating closely to our beloved

The obvious need, then, is to embrace humanity, within and without. But for that, we must thoroughly reappraise the reality, beauty, goodness, and cosmic value of what is created in human beings. And as human beings, this requires a radical recognition, re-evaluation, a comprehensive revision of our views and teachings regarding human nature.

HUMANITY ACCORDING TO EGO

The ego's position on who you are, and on being yourself, boils down to this:

"As a rule, don't be who you are. Most of the qualities of your person-hood are bad. Therefore, if people are allowed to see those qualities, they will reject you. With respect to the good qualities of your person-hood, those positive inclinations are dangerous. If you live beautifully, you will be hurt (taken advantage of, abused, mocked, despised and rejected) and you will hurt others as well. You can protect yourself from many dangers by not being yourself."

Unfortunately, most people on earth believe ego's false alarms and trumped up evidence against humanity. And it's easy to see why; as usually lived, human life is challenging. No wonder people hesitate to live as we are.

But honestly, is that a mess, a valid argument against living beautifully? No! Don't let the ego fool you! That's not who we are; it is the disastrous result of believing the ego's negative notions about who we are, who others are, and so on. What this is saying is; in trying to build a case against humanity, ego is really building a case against itself! Aberrant behavior doesn't prove the dangers of being truly' authentically human it only proves that thinking or acting in a manner consistent with the false and distorted ego's image of who we are creates pain and misfortune.

Humans biggest source of inner conflict comes from our misunderstanding about who we are. As long as we believe we have a lower part, and a higher part, a good part, and a bad part we are bound to feel inner conflict, frequently. For example. We may think "to do what my heart want, I need to fight against what my ego wants." However, whenever we've been at higher levels of self-recognition and self-acceptance, we've all enjoyed blissful relief from inner conflicts. At those times we know beyond the shadow of a doubt: "What I am is good. What I want is beautiful."

HOW EGO AVOIDS RIGHT ACTION

Left to its own devices, ego avoids right action in one of two ways: egotistical idleness, or egotistical activity. Ego often recommends retreat in cases where engagement would be more appropriate. And when ego recommends engagement, the forms of action it recommends are mostly self-centered, and therefore done in a poor spirit. Ego doesn't care which choice we take – either inaction or poor-spirited action. Either choice aborts our true mission on earth: true, divinely inspired loving, and generous hearted giving. Truly good action.

Poor-spirited action: One form of poor-spirited action is to act selfishly and insensitively. You see this everywhere: Under the influence of ego, workers tend to become greedy and competitive. Couples suffer from seemingly endless conflicts and power struggles. No wonder so many aspects of ordinary life seem complicated. Ego makes people act and react in ways that are certainly problematic.

Inaction: As part of its passivity sales pitch, ego reminds us how easily we can hurt ourselves and others whenever we take action. (And it hopes we don't remember that egotism in action is what causes the pain.)

Ordinarily, and as a matter of human tendency, the quality of people's participation in ordinary life is strongly influenced by ego. And inevitably, ego-influenced action creates wrongdoing and guilt, aversions and attachments. Given those patterns, we may reasonably wonder if it's possible to live an ordinary life without bringing ourselves and others down. And of course, we don't want to endlessly repeat mistakes! So we may conclude that we – and everyone around us – will be better off if we simply avoid certain activities and situations. There may be something laudable – even wise – about the decision not to act to avoid making a mess.

HOW TO ACT IN THE RIGHT SPIRIT

Obviously, in order to get and stay in the right spirit, we must constantly let go of the relatively poor spirit in which we as ego-identified beings tend to do (or avoid doing) things. But paradoxically, although the Way of Undoing is about getting rid of ego in our actions, we can't remove our ego obstructions by self-consciously focusing on them – or even by focusing on our effort to remove them. Excessive self-focus in any form only tends to reinforce ego identification.

Luckily, the path of right action gives us a safer, surer way up the mountain! If we accept right action as our star, we have a practical and truly effective way to defy the ego consistently. When we focus on doing something good – like loving or serving in a truly good spirit, we natural encounter our ego obstructions, as an illuminating "side-effect" of our good-spirited efforts. Especially at first, nearly every attempt to engage rightly in action requires us to transcend our selfish habits and overcome our egoic resistance. And that gives us plenty of chances to release it without reinforcing it. So it's crucial, that we embrace the challenge of right action. It is essential that we try to act as rightly and unselfishly as possible, bringing real consciousness and care to the spirit in which we act.

Clearly, a lot of people feel disillusioned and disappointed with their lives – and deeply crave something better. But when, despite the misery of it, you accept a hum-drum life, or you allow yourself to be consumed by the difficulties resulting from the way you presently live, your heart ,mind, and entire body urges for liberation remains on the back burner. An ego-transcending life can never be a matter of merely accepting a dogma or practicing a technique; it is an all-consuming commitment. Similarly, an ego-transcending life requires no special circumstances, nor is it prevented by any circumstances. It can be expressed in anything and everything we do.

HUMANS ARE GOOD

Badness and separation of man are both false ideas. Man is never bad, and never separate. However, man believes that he is separate. And, he also believes that he is bad. Therefore, based on his belief that he is bad, he tries to become good. And, based on his belief that he is separate, he considers himself on a mission to attain true goodness, as a separate individual, forming and molding his separate self into what he considers to be good.

Man's idea of goodness. If man thinks that he is separate and bad, then he also has an idea of what goodness is, an idea that is false. The truth is, man is inherently good. But if he thinks he is separate and bad, then he thinks goodness is something to be attained, apart from what he is, and different from what he is.

Based on this belief, man has created for himself a set of ideas that he calls "goodness." Many of these ideas are truly good. Man knows, for example, that love and compassion are good. Yet, he does not know that they cannot be achieved by trying, as a "separate" and "bad" person, to become "good." The result of this will only be a learned character, a learned behavior, all with effort.

As man comes to see who he really is, he will know the truth of all of existence. He will see "others" as himself, and love all. He will feel himself to be an expression of light. and will naturally pour forth love, and feel care for all of life creation. He will feel connected to and responsible for all that is; for all that exists is his own.

HUMAN CREATES THEIR OWN LIFE

The power to heal, to hurt, to grow, to diminish. Power. Huge power. Huge force. Huge changers we are, creators of huge change.

Who does not create their life? Everyone, in fact, creates their life. In one way or another, the vision of the heart creates one's life. It begins on the inside, and the potency of what is felt and born there on the inside begins to bear fruit, begins to show signs of life. It shows up in one's attitudes, in one's choices, in one's allegiances and alliances. It shows up as a string of choices that lead to other choices and opportunities. As creators, that is how we create.

All humans wishes for a life that is truly blessed and possible, beautiful and holy, provided for and whole, a life that would be worthy of all, a life that would and will summon the heart of man into higher, brighter things. You can fulfill your heart's need for a purposeful life. It's there for you, if you allow your hearts to embrace it.

May we not forget that for all of these beautiful qualities to be manifest, we need to allow ourselves to be needy for answers to life, to be confused and not knowing, to bungle around without an answer for long enough to make an impression on the universe. We need to allow ourselves to be so bold as to feel what we feel in our hearts, and desire what we desire, and seek for guidance, seek for understanding; to be vulnerable, be a sap, an ignorant, an idiot. We need all these things to be manifest, if the beauty of our hearts is to flourish and live a life you value.

The truth of who we are is evident. Nothing can prevent us from breaking free, and learning the truth in the school of our own life experience. All that's in the way are a few false beliefs and expectations. So arise and rightly use your human qualities and live as totally as you are.

COLORFUL LIFE

Color has power. Colors may excite, express happiness, show signs of grieve, make us look blissful. Color is now so much part of our everyday lives and our society that without it, we would literally be living in a boring , bland and sad world.

Colors transform our environment, colors by absorbing through our skin by wearing make up or tattoos, make our life rich and beautiful. Colors have an enormous effect on our emotions, physical, and mental health it is a real celebration of life.

Egyptians from centuries ago used colors positively, for a profound healing quality. We can use colors constructively to enhance our well-being, improve our lives and discover more about ourselves at the same time.

Every color has its own energy. Our attraction to various colors may signal areas where we are balanced or imbalanced. Some colors may connect with you, some may not.

THE HISTORY OF COLOR

Color and light have always been an essential part of life and our existence of earth. One of the earliest records of the magical powers of color can been seen in Lascaux and Altimara where decorative paintings of various animals adorn the interior cave walls. In Lascaux and Altimara the calcite crystals that sparkle and lime the cave walls introduced white into the paintings to create and produce subtle shades and effective perspectives.

Human's soon realized the importance of color with the changes of colors in nature, the cycle of day into night, when the sun set a red dusk indicated the end of daily activity. Red and black are the colors symbolic of life and death. They were first used to decorate the graves of the deceased and later the same colors were used by their ancestors to adorn their first works of art.

From the moment we wake up each day our eyes are filled with various colors . We can use the power of colors to influence others and to make ourselves more persuasive, understanding another person's personality, and how colors affects our mood. We also use colors for buildings and self-decoration, such as body painting, found among tribal communities.

A lot of people adorn themselves with a variety of colored make-up, usually on the face. Women wear make-up to alter the shape and appearance of their features, enhancing their natural coloring at the same time, and performers use it to create the best and most striking effects under the the strongest of lighting.

SOME COLORS AND WHAT THEY REPRESENTS

The color Blue is associated with trust, divinity, truth, integrity, loyalty. So the simple act of wearing Blue can influence others to trust you more.

The color Red signifies strength, high energy. It can cause our heart rate to increase in speed. When process through the retina and into usu-able brain signals our subconscious mind associate Red with danger.

The color Green represents calmness, relaxation, clear visions. Just remind yourself how peaceful and calm you feel when walking through a park or forestry of trees.

The color Yellow is flashy and summery and fills you up with optimism. Purple is for elegance, and fragrance. Pink is for kindness.

The shades Black and White which are often confused by classing it has colors. Neither of the two belong to primary or secondary colors. Black is a major and powerful shade. A few people seem to think it represents sad moments. However, its very significant effects, as it reflects power and authority. Black as got slimming effects in clothing.

The shade white signifies purity and innocence.

Colors does make human's lives very desirable, adorable, happy and meaningful.

COLOR IN HEALING

Color healing was widely practiced by the ancient Egyptians, Babylonians and Assyrians . They recognized the powerful effects of the sun ray and regularly exposed their bodies to it for healing purposes. They also recognized the significance of light and color rays contained within crystals and gemstones.

In certain parts of the world, medicines have been mixed with crushed gold and pearls for rheumatism, bronchitis and epilepsy; emeralds for diabetes; rubies for the heart and brain. In recent times there has been a huge revival of interest in crystal healing, and color visualization is a vital element in its practice.

LIFE CIRCLES

Truth is the rock foundation of every great character. It is loyalty to the right as we see it; it is courageous living of our lives in harmony with our ideals; it is always power. It is the compass of the soul, the guardian of conscience, the final touchstone of right. Truth is the revelation of the ideal; but it is also an inspiration to realize that ideal, a constant impulse to live it.

Truth can stand alone, for it needs no chaperone or escort. Lies are cowardly, fearsome things that must travel in battalions. They are like a lot of drunken men, one vainly seeking to support another. Lying is the partner and accomplice of all the other vices. It is the cancer of moral degeneracy in an individual life.

Law is the eternal truth of nature the unity that always produces identical results under identical conditions. When a man discovers a great truth in nature he has the key to the understanding of a million phenomena; when he grasps a great truth in morals he has in it the key to his spiritual re-creation. For the individual, there is no such thing as theoretic truth; a great truth that is not absorbed by our whole mind and life, and has not become an inseparable part of our living, is not a real truth to us. If we know the truth and do not live it, our life is a lie.

Truth means "that which one troweth or believes." It is living simply and squarely by our belief; it is the externalizing of a faith in a series of actions. Truth is ever strong, courageous, virile, though kindly, gentle, calm, and restful. There is a vital difference between error and untruthfulness. A man may be in error and yet live bravely by it; he who is untruthful in his life knows the truth but denies it. The one is loyal to what he believes, the other is traitor to what he knows.

Truth is ever strong, courageous, virile, though kindly, gentle, calm, and restful. There is a vital difference between error and untruthfulness. A man may be in error and yet live bravely by it; he who is untruthful in his life knows the truth but denies it. The one is loyal to what he believes, the other is traitor to what he knows.

Every new sect, every new cult, has in it a grain of truth, at least; it is this that attracts attention and wins adherents. This mustard seed of truth is often overestimated, darkening the eyes of man to the untrue parts or phases of the varying religious faiths. But, in exact proportion to the basic truth they contain do religions last, become permanent and growing, and satisfy and inspire the hearts of men. Mushrooms of error have a quick growth, but they exhaust their vitality and die, while truth still lives.

The man who makes the acquisition of wealth the goal and ultimatum of his life, seeing it as an end rather than a means to an end, is not true. Why does the world usually make wealth the criterion of success, and riches the synonym of attainment? Real success in life means the individual's conquest of himself; it means "how he has bettered himself" not "how he has bettered his fortune." The great question of life is not "What have I?" but "What am I?"

Man is usually loyal to what he most desires. The man who lies to save a nickel, merely proclaims that he esteems a nickel more than he does his honor. He who sacrifices his ideals, truth and character, for mere money or position, is weighing his conscience in one pan of a scale against a bag of gold in the other. He is loyal to what he finds the heavier, that which he desires the more the money. But this is not truth. Truth is the heart's loyalty to abstract right, made manifest in concrete instances.

It is in the trifles of daily life that truth should be our constant guide and inspiration. Truth is not a dress-suit, consecrated to special occasions, it is the strong, well-woven, durable homespun for daily living. The man who says pleasant things and makes promises which to him are light as air, but to someone else seem the rock upon which a life's hope is built is cruelly untrue. He who does not regard his appointments, carelessly breaking them or ignoring them, is the thoughtless thief of another person's time. It reveals selfishness, carelessness, and lax business morals. It is untrue to the simplest justice of life.

Men who split hairs with their conscience, who mislead others by deft, shrewd phrasing which may be true in letter yet lying in spirit and designed uttered to produce a false impression, are untruthful in the most cowardly way. Such men would cheat even in solitaire, and congratulating themselves on the cleverness of their alibi. Behind every untruth is some reason, some cause, and it is this cause that should be removed. The lie may be the result of fear, the attempt to cover a fault and to escape punishment; it may be merely the evidence of an over-active imagination; it may reveal maliciousness or obstinacy; it may be the hunger for praise that leads the child to win attention and to startle others by wonderful stories; it may be merely carelessness in speech, the reckless use of words; it may be acquisitiveness that makes lying the handmaid of theft. But if, in the life of the child or the adult, the symptom be made to reveal the disease, and that be then treated, truth reasserts itself and the moral health is restored.

The power of Truth, in its highest, purest, and most exalted phases, stands squarely on four basic lines of relation, the love of truth, the search for

GOLDEN PURPOSES OF LIFE

truth, faith in truth, and work for truth. The love of truth is the cultivated hunger for it in itself and for itself, without any thought of what it may cost, what sacrifices it may entail, what theories or beliefs of a lifetime may be laid desolate. In its supreme phase, this attitude of life is rare, but unless one can begin to put himself into harmony with this view, the individual will only creep in truth, when he might walk bravely. With the love of truth, the individual scorns to do a mean thing, no matter what be the gain, even if the whole world would approve. He would not sacrifice the sanction of his own high standard for any gain, he would not willingly deflect the needle of his thought and act from the true north, as he knows it, by the slightest possible variation. He himself would know of the deflection that would be enough. What matters it what the world thinks if he have his own disapproval?

The search for Truth means that the individual must not merely follow truth as he sees it, but he must, so far as he can, search to see that he is right. The search for truth is the angel of progress in civilization and in morals. While it makes us bold and aggressive in our own life, it teaches us to be tender and sympathetic with others. Their life may represent a station we have passed in our progress, or one we must seek to reach. We can then congratulate ourselves without condemning them. All the truths of the world are not concentrated in our creed. All the sunshine of the world is not focused on our doorstep. We should ever speak the truth, but only in love and kindness.

Faith in Truth is an essential to perfect companionship with truth. The individual must have perfect confidence and assurance of the final triumph of right, and order, and justice, and believe that all things are evolving toward that divine consummation, no matter how dark and dreary life may seem from day to day. No real success, no lasting happiness can exist except it be founded on the rock of truth. The prosperity that is based on lying, deception, and intrigue, is only temporary it cannot last any more than a mushroom can outlive an oak. No matter what price a man may pay for truth, he is getting it at a bargain. The lying of others can never hurt us long, it always carries with it our exoneration in the end.

Work for the interests and advancement of Truth is a necessary part of real companionship. If a man has a love of truth, if he searches to find it, and has faith in it, even when he cannot find it, will he not work to spread it? The strongest way for man to strengthen the power of truth in the world is to live it himself in every detail of thought, word, and deed to make himself a sun of personal radiation of truth, and to let his silent influence speak for it and his direct acts glorify it so far as he can in his sphere of life and action. Let him first seek to be, before he seeks to teach or to do, in any line of moral growth.

Let man realize that Truth is essentially an intrinsic virtue, in his relation to himself even if there were no other human being living; it becomes extrinsic as he radiates it in his daily life. Truth is first, intellectual honesty the craving to know the right; second, it is moral honesty, the hunger to live the right.

Truth is not a mere absence of the vices. This is only a moral vacuum. Truth is the living, pulsing breathing of the virtues of life. Mere refraining from wrong-doing is but keeping the weeds out of the garden of one's life. But this must be followed by positive planting of the seeds of right to secure the flowers of true living. If you have Truth on your side you can pass through the dark valley of slander, misrepresentation and abuse, undaunted, as though you wore a magic suit of mail that no bullet could enter, no arrow could pierce. You can hold your head high, toss it fearlessly and defiantly, look every man calmly and unflinchingly in the eye, as though you rode, a victorious king, with banners waving and lances glistening, and bugles filling the air with music. You can feel the great expansive wave of moral health surging through you as the quickened blood courses through the body of him who is gladly, gloriously proud of physical health. You will know that all will come right in the end, that it must come, that error must flee before the great white light of truth, as darkness slinks away into nothingness in the presence of the sunburst. Then, with truth as your guide, your companion, your ally, and inspiration, you tingle with the consciousness of your kinship with the infinite and all the petty trials, sorrows and sufferings of life fade away like temporary, harmless visions seen in a dream.

LIFE CONQUEST

This world can be a delightful place to live in. However, man's worst enemy is always man. The greater part of the pain, sorrow and misery in life is purely a human invention, yet man, with cowardly irreverence, dares to throw the responsibility on mother nature. It comes through breaking laws, laws natural, physical, civic, mental or moral. These are laws which man knows, but he disregards; he takes chances; he thinks he can dodge results in some way. But nature says, "He who breaks, pays." There are no dead-letter laws on the divine statute-books of life.

Nine tenths of the world's sorrow, misfortune and unhappiness is preventable. Sometimes it is carelessness, inattention, neglect of duty, avarice, anger, jealousy, dissipation, betrayal of trust, selfishness, hypocrisy, revenge, dishonesty, any of a hundred phases of the preventable.

That which can be prevented, should be prevented. It all rests with the individual. The "preventable" exists in three degrees: First, that which is due to the individual solely and directly; second, that which he suffers through the wrong-doing of those around him, other individuals; third, those instances wherein he is the unnecessary victim of the wrongs of society, the innocent legatee of the folly of humanity and society is but the massing of thousands of individuals with the heritage of manners, customs and laws they have received from the past.

We sometimes feel heart-sick and weary in facing failure, when the fortune that seemed almost in our fingers slips away because of the envy, malice or treachery of some one else. We bow under the weight of a sorrow that makes all life grow dark and the star of hope fade from our vision; or we meet some unnecessary misfortune with a dumb, helpless despair. "It is all wrong," we say, "it is cruel, it is unjust. Why is it permitted?" And, in the very intensity of our feeling, we half-unconsciously repeat the words over and over again, in monotonous iteration, as if in some way the very repetition might bring relief, might somehow soothe us. Yet, in most instances, it could be prevented. No suffering is caused in the world by right. Whatever sorrow there is that is preventable, comes from in harmony or wrong of some kind.

In the divine economy of the universe most of the evil, pain and suffering are unnecessary, even when overruled for good, and perhaps, if our knowledge were perfect, it would be seen that none is necessary, that all is preventable. The fault is mine, or yours, or the fault of the world. It is always individual. The world itself is but the cohesive united force of the thoughts, words and deeds of millions who have lived or who are living, like you and me. By individuals has the great wrong that causes our preventable sorrow been built up, by individuals must it be weakened and transformed to right. And in this, too, it is to a great degree our fault; we care so little about rousing public sentiment, of lashing it into activity unless it concerns us individually.

Most accidents are preventable. When a terrible fire makes a city desolate and a nation mourn, the investigation that follows usually shows that a little human foresight could have prevented it, or at least, lessened the horror of it all. If chemicals or dynamite are stored in any building in excess of what wise legislation declares is safe, some one has been cruelly careless. Perhaps it is some inspector who has been disloyal to his trust, by permitting bribes to chloroform his sense of duty. If the lack of fire-escapes adds its quota to the list of deaths, or if the avarice of the owner has made his building a fire-trap, public feeling becomes intense, the newspapers are justly loud in their protests, and in demands that the guilty ones be punished. "If the laws already on the statute books do not cover the situation," we hear from day to day, "new laws will be framed to make a repetition of the tragedy impossible"; we are promised all kinds of reforms; the air seems filled with a spirit of regeneration; the mercury of public indignation rises to the point where "fever-heat" seems a mild, inadequate term.

Then, as the horror begins to fade in the perspective of the past, men go quietly back to their own personal cares and duties, and the mighty wave of righteous protest that threatened so much, dies in gentle lapping on the shore. What has been all men concern seems soon to concern no one. The tremendous energy of the authorities seems like the gesture of a drunken man, that starts from his shoulder with a force that would almost fell an ox but when it reaches the hand it has expended itself, and the hand drops listlessly in the air with hardly power enough to disturb the serenity of a butterfly. There is always a little progress, a slight advance, and it is only the constant accumulation of these steps that is giving to the world greater dominion over the preventable.

Constant vigilance is the price of the conquest of the preventable. We have no right to admit any wrong or evil in the world as necessary, until we have exhausted every precaution that human wisdom can suggest to prevent it. Poverty has no necessary place in life. It is a disease that results from the weakness, sin, and selfishness of humanity. Nature is boundless in her generosity; the world produces sufficient to give food, clothing, and comfort to every individual. Poverty is preventable. Poverty may result from the shiftlessness, idleness, intemperance, improvidence, lack of purpose or evil-doing of the individual himself.

If the causes do not exist in the individual, they may be found in the second class, in the wrong-doing of those around him, in the oppression of labor by capital, in the grinding process by which corporations seek to crush the individual. The individual may be the victim of any of a thousand phases of the wrong of others. The poverty caused by the third class, the weakness and injustice of human laws and human institutions, is also preventable, but to reach the cause requires time and united heroic effort of all individuals.

The world is learning the great truth, that the best way to prevent crime is to study the sociologic conditions in which it flourishes, to seek to give each man a better chance of living his real life by removing, if possible, the elements that make wrong easy, and to him, almost necessary, and by inspiring him to fight life's battle bravely with all the help others can give him. It is so much wiser to prevent than to cure; to keep some one from being burned is so much better than89 inventing new poultices for unnecessary hurts.

Let the individual say each day, as he rises new-created to face a new life: "Today no one in the world shall suffer because I live. I will be kind, considerate, careful in thought and speech and act. I will seek to discover the element that weakens me as a power in the world, and that keeps me from living up to the fullness of my possibility. That weakness I will master today. I will conquer it, at any cost."

The world needs societies formed of members pledged to the individual conquest of preventable pain and sorrow. The individual has no right that runs counter to the right of any one else. There are no solo parts in the eternal music of life. Each must pour out his life in duo with every other. Every moment must be one of choice, of good or of evil. Which will the individual choose? His life will be his answer. Let him dedicate his life to making the world around him brighter, sweeter and better, and by his conquest of preventable pain and sorrow he will day by day get fuller revelation of the glory of the possibilities of individual living, and come nearer and nearer to the realization of his ideals.

HAVING AIMS IN LIFE CIRCLES
It is the aim that makes the man, and without this he is nothing as far as the utter destitution of force,

weight, and even individuality among men can reduce him to nonentity. Take heed, young man, of an aimless life. Take heed, too, of a low and sordid aim. A well-ascertained and generous purpose gives vigor, direction, and perseverance to all man's efforts. Its concomitants are a well-disciplined intellect, character, influence, tranquility, and cheerfulness within success and honor without. Whatever a man's talents and advantages may be, with no aim, or a low one, he is weak and despicable; and he can not be otherwise than respectable and influential with a high one. Without some definite object before us, some standard which we are earnestly striving to reach, we can not expect to attain to any great height, either mentally or morally. Placing for ourselves high standards, and wishing to reach them without any further effort on our part, is not enough to elevate us in any very great degree.

To live for something worthy of life involves the necessity of an intelligent and definite plan of action. More than splendid dreaming or magnificent resolves is necessary to success in the objects and ambitions of life. Men come to the best results in every department of effort only as they thoughtfully plan and earnestly toil in given directions. Purposes without work is dead. It were vain to hope for good results from mere plans. Random or spasmodic efforts, like aimless shoots, are generally no better than wasted time or strength. The purposes of shrewd men in the business of this life are always followed by careful plans, enforced by work. Whether the object is learning, honor, or wealth, the ways and means are always laid out according to the best rules and methods. The mariner has his chart, the architect his plans, the sculptor his model, and all as a means and condition of success. Inventive genius, or even what is called inspiration, can do little in any department of the theoretic or practical science except as it works by a well-formed plan; then every step is an advance towards the accomplishment of its object. Every tack of the ship made in accordance with nautical law keeps her steadily nearing the port. Each stroke of the chisel brings the marble into a clearer likeness to the model. No effort or time is lost; for nothing is done rashly or at random.

Thus, in the grand aim of life, if some worthy purpose be kept constantly in view, and for its accomplishment every effort be made every day of your life, you will, unconsciously, perhaps, approach the goal of your ambition. That fixed of purpose is a grand element of human success. When a man has formed in his mind a great sovereign purpose, it governs his conduct as the laws of nature govern the operation of physical things.

Every one should have a mark in view, and pursue it steadily. He should not be turned from his course by other objects ever so attractive. Life is not long enough for any one man to accomplish every thing. Indeed, but few can at best accomplish more than one thing well. Many accomplish nothing. Yet there is not a man, endowed with ordinary intellect or accomplishments, but can accomplish at least one useful, important, worthy purpose. It was not without reason that some of the greatest of men were trained from their youth to choose some definite object in life, to which they were required to direct their thoughts and to devote all their energies. It became, therefore, a sole and ruling purpose of their hearts, and was almost certainly the means of their future advancement and happiness in the world.

Of the thousands of men who are annually coming upon the stage of life there are few who escape the necessity of adopting some profession or calling; and there are fewer still who, if they knew the miseries of idleness tenfold keener and more numerous than those of the most laborious profession would ever desire such an escape. First of all, a choice of business or occupation should be made, and made early, with a wise reference to capacity and taste. The youth should be educated for it and, as far as possible, in it; and when this is done it should be pursued with industry, energy, and enthusiasm, which will warrant success.

This choice of an occupation depends partly upon the individual preference and partly upon circumstances. It may be that you are debarred from entering upon that business for which you are best adapted. In that case make the best choice in your power, apply yourself faithfully and earnestly to whatever you undertake, and you can not well help achieving a success. Patient application sometimes leads to great results. No man should be discouraged because he does not get on rapidly in his calling from the start. In the more intellectual professions especially it should be remembered that a solid character is not the growth of a day, that the mental faculties are not matured except by long and laborious culture.

You will receive all sorts of the most excellent advice, but you must do your own deciding. You have to take care of yourself in this world, and you may as well take your own way of doing it. But if a change of business is desired be sure the fault is with the business and not the individual. For running hither and thither generally makes sorry work, and brings to poverty ere the sands of life are half run. The continents on earth furnish vast fields for enterprise; but of what avail for the seeker to visit the four corners of the world if he still is dissatisfied, and returns home with empty pockets and idle hands, thinking that the world is wrong and that he himself is a misused and shamefully imposed-on creature? The world, smiling at the rebuff, moves on, while he lags behind, groaning over misusage, without sufficient energy to roll up his sleeves and fight his way through.

Always remember that it is not your trade or profession that makes you respectable. Manhood and profession or handicraft are entirely different things. An occupation is never an end of life. It is an instrument put into our hands by which to gain for the body the means of living until sickness or old age robs it of life, and we pass on to the world for which this is a preparation. The great purpose of living is twofold in character. The one should never change from the time reason takes the helm; it is to live a life of manliness, of purity and honor. To live such a life that, whether rich or poor, your neighbors will honor and respect you as a man of sterling principles. The other is to have some business, in the due performance of which you are to put forth all your exertions. It matters not so much what it is as whether it be honorable, and it may change to suit the varying change of circumstances. When these two objects character and a high aim are fairly before a youth, what then? He must strive to attain those objects. He must work as well as dream, labor as well as pray. His hand must be as stout as his heart, his arm as strong as his head. Purpose must be followed by action. Then is he living and acting worthily, as becomes a human being with great destinies in store for him.

Many of you today are just starting on the duties of an active life. The volume of the future lies unopened before you. Its covers are illuminated by the pictures of fancy, and its edges are gleaming with the golden tints of hope. Man may make life what he pleases and give it as much worth, both for himself and others, as he has energy for.

The journey is a laborious one, and you must not expect to find the road all smooth. And whether rich or poor, high or low, you will be disappointed if you build on any other foundation. Take life like a man; take it just as though it was as it is an earnest, vital, essential affair. Take it just as though you personally were born to the task of performing a merry part in it as though the world had waited for your coming. Live for something, and for something worthy of life and its capabilities and opportunities, for noble deeds and achievements. Every man and every woman has his or her assignments in the duties and responsibilities of daily life. We are in the world to make the world better, to lift it up to higher levels of enjoyment and progress, to make the hearts and homes brighter and happier by devoting to our fellows our best thoughts, activities, and influences.

Life embraces in its comprehensiveness a just return of failure and success as the result of individual perseverance and labor. Live for something definite and practical; take hold of things with a will, and they will yield to you and become the ministers of your own happiness and that of others. Nothing within the realm of the possible can withstand the man or woman who is intelligently bent on success. Every person carries within the key that unlocks either door of success or failure. Which shall it be? All desire success; the problem of life is its winning.

Strength, bravery, dexterity, and unfaltering nerve and resolution must be the portion and attribute of those who resolve to pursue fortune along the rugged road of life. Their path will often lie amid rocks and crags, and not on lawns and among lilies. A great action is always preceded by a great purpose. History and daily life are full of examples to show us that the measure of human achievements has always been proportional to the amount of human daring and doing. Deal with questions and facts of life as they really are. What can be done, and is worth doing, do with dispatch; what can not be done, or would be worthless when done, leave for the idlers and dreamers along life's highway.

Life often presents us with a choice of evils instead of good; and if any one would get through life honorably and peacefully he must learn to bear as well as forbear, to hold the temper in subjection to the judgment, and to practice self-denial in small as well as great things. Human life is a watch-tower. the young especially, should take their stand on this tower, to look, listen, learn, wherever they go and wherever they tarry. Life is short, and yet for you it may be long enough to lose your character, your constitution, or your estate; or, on the other hand, by diligence you can accomplish much within its limits.

If the man of genius can create work in life that shall speak the triumph of mind a thousand years hence, then may true men and women, alive to the duty and obligations of existence, do infinitely more. Working on human hearts and destinies, it is their prerogative to do imperishable work, to build within life's fleeting hours monuments that shall last forever. If such grand possibilities lie within the reach of our personal actions in the world how important that we live for something every hour of our existence, and for something that is harmonious with the dignity of our present being and the grandeur of our future destiny!

A steady aim, with a strong arm, willing hands, and a resolute will, are the necessary requisites to the conflict which begins anew each day and writes upon the scroll of yesterday the actions that form one mighty column where from true worth is estimated. One day's work left undone causes a break in the great chain that years of toil may not be able to repair. Yesterday was ours, but it is gone; today is all we possess, for tomorrow we may never see; therefore, in the golden hour of the present the seeds are planted whereby the harvest for good or evil is to be reaped.

To endure with cheerfulness, hoping for little, asking for much, is, perhaps, the true plan. Decide at once upon a noble purpose, then take it up bravely, bear it off joyfully, lay it down triumphantly. Be industrious, be frugal, be honest, deal with kindness with all who come in your way, and if you do not prosper as rapidly as you would wish depend upon it you will be happy.

The web of life is drawn into the loom for us, but we weave it ourselves. We throw our own shuttle and work our own treadle. The warp is given us, but the woof we furnish find our own materials, and color and figure it to suit ourselves. Every man is the architect of his own house, his own temple of fame. If he builds one great, glorious, and honorable, the merit and the bliss are his; if he rears a polluted, unsightly, vice-haunted den, to himself the shame and misery belongs.

Life is often but a bitter struggle from first to last with many who wear smiling faces and are ever ready with a cheerful word, when there is scarcely a shred left of the hopes and opportunities which for years promised happiness and content. But it is human still to strive and yearn and grope for some unknown good that shall send all unrest and troubles to the winds and settle down over one's life with a halo of peace and satisfaction. The rainbow of hope is always visible in the future. Life is like a winding lane, on either side bright flowers and tempting fruits, which we scarcely pause to admire or taste, so eager are we to pass to an opening in the distance, which we imagine will be more beautiful; but, alas! we find we have only hastened by these tempting scenes to arrive at a desert waste.

We creep into childhood, bound into youth, sober into manhood, and totter into old age. But through all let us so live that when in the evening of life the golden clouds rest sweetly and invitingly upon the golden mountains, and the light of heaven streams down through the gathering mists of death, we may have a peaceful and joyous entrance into that world of blessedness, where the great riddle of life, whose meaning we can only guess at, will be unfolded to us in the quick consciousness of a soul redeemed and purified.

POWER

The things of the world are fluid to a power within man by which he rules them. You need not acquire this power. You already have it. But you want to understand it; you want to use it; you want to control it, so that you can go forward and carry the world before you. Day by day as you go on and on, as you gain momentum, as your inspiration deepens, as your plans crystallize, as you gain understanding, you will come to realize that this world is no dead pile of stones and timber, but that it is a living thing! It is made up of the beating hearts of humanity.

It is a thing of life and beauty. It is evident that it requires understanding to work with material of this description, but those who come into this understanding, are inspired by a new light, a force, they gain confidence and grater power each day, they realize their hopes and dreams come true, life as a deeper, fuller, clearer meaning than ever before.

The powers, uses and possibilities of the mind under the new interpretations are in comparably more wonderful that the most extravagant accomplishment, or even dreams of material progress.

Thought is energy. Active thought is active energy; concentrated thought is a concentrated energy. Thought concentrated on a definite purpose become power. This is the power to which is being used by those who do not believe in virtue of poverty, or the beauty of self-denial. They perceived that it is the talk of weaklings.

The ability to receive and manifest this power depends upon the ability to recognize the infinite energy ever dwelling in man, constantly creating and recreating his bod and mind, and ready at any moment to manifest through him in any needful manner. In exact proportion to the recognition of this truth will be the manifestation in the outer life of the individual.

Eliminate, therefore, any possible tendency to complain of conditions as they have been, or as they are, because it rests with you to change them and make them what you would like them to be. Direct your efforts to a realization of the mental resources, always at your command, from which real lasting power comes.

Persist in this practice until you come to a realization of the fact that there can be no failure in the accomplishment of any proper object in life if you but understand your power to persist in your object, because the mind-focus are ever ready to lend themselves to a purposeful will, in the effort to crystallize thought and desire into actions, events, and conditions.

Thoughts alone works no magic transformations; it obeys natural laws; it sets in motion natural forces; it releases natural energies; it manifests in your conduct and actions, and these in turn react upon your friends and acquaintances, and eventually upon the whole of your environment. You can originate thought, and, since thoughts are creative, you can create for yourself things you desire.

Our life is a continual oscillation between our share in the universal world-process and our own individual existence. The farther we ascend into the universal nature of thought where the individual, at last, interests us only as an example, an instance, of the concept, the more the character of something individual, of the quite determinate, unique personality, becomes lost in us. The farther we descend into the depths of our own private life and allow the vibrations of our feelings to accompany all our experiences of the outer world, the more we cut ourselves off from the universal life. True individuality belongs to him whose feelings reach up to the farthest possible extent into the region of the ideal. There are men in whom even the most general ideas still bear that peculiar personal tinge which shows unmistakably their connection with their author. There are others whose concepts come before us as devoid of any trace of individual colouring as if they had not been produced by a being of flesh and blood at all.

A life of feeling, wholly devoid of thought, would gradually lose all connection with the world. But man is meant to be a whole, and knowledge of objects will go hand-in-hand for him with the development and education of the feeling-side of his nature. Feeling is the means whereby, in the first instance, concepts gain concrete life.

LIFE NATURE

Normally we say that the purpose of life is happiness. This means that our duty as thinkers is to watch life, to test it, to pick and choose among the many forms it offers, and to say: This kind of growth is more permanent and full of promise, it is more fertile, more deeply satisfactory; therefore, we choose this, and sanction the kind of pleasure which it brings. Other kinds we decide are temporary and delusive.

It is perfectly true that human reason is fallible. Infallibility is an absolute, a concept of the mind, and not a reality. Life has not given us infallibility, any more than it has given us omniscience, or omnipotence, or any other of those attributes which we call divine. Life has given us powers, more or less weak, more or less strong, but all capable of improvement and development. Reason is the tool whereby mankind has won supremacy over the rest of the animal kingdom, and is gradually taking control of the forces of nature. It is the best tool we have, and because it is the best, we are driven irresistibly to use it.

Man is a part of nature and a product of nature; in many fundamental respects his ways are still nature's ways and his laws still nature's laws. But there are other and even more significant ways in which man has separated himself from nature and made himself something quite different.

A consideration of all the facts leads us to the result that a life consisting solely of nature and intelligence involves an intolerable inconsistency: form and content are sharply separated from each other; thought is strong enough to disturb the sense of satisfaction with nature, but is too weak to construct a new world in opposition to it.

The experience of our time confirms this conclusion in no indefinite manner. Since, with regard to the material and the technical, we have attained heights never before reached, the bonds between us and our environment have increased a thousandfold, and our work has united us more closely with the world, we seem now for the first time to attain a sure hold of reality. At the same time, however, the activity of thought, and with it unrestrained reflection, have also increased immeasurably in modern life. The emergence of a new life, which can do nothing but comprehend the other in thought, and which, while it is indeed capable of depreciating the other, cannot itself advance further, is seen to involve a monstrous inconsistency.

If the union of nature and intelligence produces so much confusion, we are inevitably led to ask whether man does not possess in himself more than thought; whether thought is not rooted in a deeper and a more comprehensive life, from which it derives its power. It is not necessary that such a life should be manifest to us in all its completeness; we shall also be compelled to acknowledge it as a fact even if in the first place it has to struggle up in face of opposition; however, in its development it must show distinctive contents and powers which could not be the work of a subjective reflection. If there is a life and a development of this kind, it will be necessary for us to comprehend it in its various aspects and tendencies, and only when we have accomplished this may we endeavour to obtain a representation of the whole.

Even in a "state of nature" man takes his family, his nation, and the whole of humanity indeed, up into his interests; and as this tendency is not bounded from without, but may be immeasurably refined and extended in an indefinite number of directions, it easily comes to appear that this involves an inner deliverance from self, and that another is of value to us for his own sake. But it is no more than an appearance; for with all the external agreement the inward separation is far greater, and amounts to opposition. Within the limits of nature we can certainly concern ourselves with something which is only indirectly useful to us; but we can never be concerned with anything which is devoid of all use to ourselves; we cannot take such a direct interest in the welfare of others as will tend to our own disadvantage. If experience gives evidence of such an activity and such an interest, in so doing it demonstrates a transcendence of nature.

The social life of man is not explicable as a simple collection of individuals related to one another in different ways; but in the family, in the state, in humanity as a whole there is evolved an inner unity, a sphere of life with distinctive values and contents. And as it is of the nature of these to transcend the ends and aims of the individuals, to arouse other feelings and stimulate to other efforts, so their demands may be directly opposed to those of individual self-preservation. Man sees himself compelled to decide whether he will pursue his own welfare or that of the whole: from the necessity of a decision it is impossible to escape. However much in the majority of cases self-interest may preponderate, we cannot dispute the possibility of his acting in direct and conscious opposition to his own interest; of his subordinating and sacrificing himself; and of his doing this "not grudgingly nor of necessity," but willingly and gladly; of his feeling this subordination to be not a negation and a limitation, but an affirmation and an expansion of his life

All who strive for some essential renewal and elevation of human life base their hope and trust upon such a disposition. A renewal and an elevation of life involve far too much toil, conflict, and danger; they demand a renunciation 121 and a sacrifice far too great for them to be commended to us by consideration of our own welfare, or for them to dispense with the necessity of counting upon an unselfish submission, a sincere sympathy, a genuine love. How much real love and genuine sympathy the experience of humanity shows is a question in itself. Even as possibilities of our being, as matters of thought which occupy our attention, and as tasks and problems, they give evidence of a development of our life beyond the limits of nature.

USING OUR TALENTS

Everyone's got a talent. There is a truly, remarkable, magical feeling to use our talents for positive outcomes.

Some people never use their talents, others use their talents at an early or later years of their lives.

Here is an example, I would like to share with you, of a person name Hayley who has used her talents and she's now enjoying a happy life.

EXAMPLE

On a clear bright morning, scattered fluffy clouds floated in the sky. I was on my way to the local newsagent to buy a newspaper. Kind and caring parents were taking their little children to school, busy people were rushing to work, two scruffy looking men across the road standing by the bus stop, staring at Hayley shook their heads clear of pleasant visions.

Just before I entered the newsagent, my face blossomed when I caught a glance at Hayley gliding towards me. A few of her curly blonde hairs swished across her forehead and glowed radiantly in the morning sun.

Hayley greeted me "Hello my little jelly, teddy. I'm going to the Yates for a coffee, care to join me? I've got some fantastic news I'd like to share with you."

I quickly dashed into the newsagent and got my newspaper.

As we walked into the Yates, the sight and smell of cooked breakfast made my stomach rumble, reminding me that I'd not eaten since seven p.m. the previous day.

Hayley and I, then reached towards the counter. Two bar staff. One had broad, muscled shoulders, with a natural steamrolling style. The other tall and slim with a light ginger stubble on his chin, both gravitated towards Hayley like bees to honey to take Hayley's order.

I ogled the painted coffee sign on the mug of coffee covered with a smiley face. Hayley started to share her wonderful news with me.

HAYLEY

I started up a tattoo shop at a moment in my life where a choice had to be made. I was made redundant from my job, no regular money coming in but I had a choice. From a young age I've always enjoyed drawing pictures and paintings.

I decided to use my talent and went to college, got qualification in fine arts. It was a life changing and best decision I've ever made. With the help of positive steps I opened up a tattoo shop.

Being a tattoo artist allowed me to use my creative side. I loved when a customer recommend other people to the shop. These customers always instilled in me a love for the designs and various colors of tattoos they wear on their skin.

The shop opens six days per week. Right now there are four tattooists working in the shop, and we are always booked solid for up to two weeks in advance. We host guest artist which give the shop an exciting atmosphere.

I now have a desire to open another tattoo shop soon. The only challenging part of my work is the long hours, has I like to keep my customers happy.

WISDOM/SELF-KNOWLEDGE

As soon as beauty is known by the world as beautiful, it becomes ugly.

As soon as virtue is being known as something good, it becomes evil.

Is the Beautiful without us, or is it not rather within us? What we call sweet and bitter is our own sweetness, our own bitterness, for nothing can be sweet or bitter without us. Is it not the same with the Beautiful? The world is like a rich mine, full of precious ore, but each man has to assay the ore for himself, before he knows what is gold and what is not. What, then, is the touchstone by which we assay the Beautiful? We have a touchstone for discovering the good. Whatever is unselfish is good. But—though nothing can be beautiful, except what is in some sense or other good, not everything that is good is also beautiful. What, then, is that something which, added to the good, makes it beautiful.

When success is achieved, he seeks no recognition.

Because he does not claim for the credit, hence shall not lose it.

By not adoring the worthy, people will not fall into dispute.

By not valuing the hard to get objects, people will not become robbers.

By not seeing the desires of lust, one's heart will not be confused. Therefore the governing of the saint is to empty one's mind, substantiate one's virtue, weakens one's worldly ambition and strengthen one's essence.

He lets the people to be innocent of worldly knowledge and desire, and keeps the clever ones from making trouble with their wits.

Acts naturally without desire, then everything will be accomplished in its natural order.

He who wishes to take control of the world and acts upon it, I can see that he will not succeed. For the world is a divine vessel, it cannot be acted upon as one wish.

He who acts on it fails. He who holds on to it loses. Therefore some things move forward while some follow behind. Some try to warm with exhaled air while some try to blow it cold.

Some are strong while some are weak. Some are successfully accomplished while some are declined and failed. Thus, the saint avoids all extremes, extravagance, and pride.

Great achievement appears to be inadequate, yet its use is never exhausted.

Great fullness appears to be void, yet its use is boundless. Great honesty may seem to be accused of wrong doing.

Great mastery appears to be clumsy.

Great eloquence may seem to be articulate.

Movement can overcome chill. Tranquility can overcome heat. Peace and calmness is the way to guide the world.

There is nothing in this world that is softer and meeker than water. Even those that can conquer the strong and the hard, are still not superior than water nothing can substitute it.

Hence, what is soft can overcome the strong.

What is gentle can overcome the strength. This is known by the world. However, people cannot put it into practice.

Therefore, the saint said as follow: He who can take the disgrace of a nation, is said to be the master of the nation.

There is certainly no happier life than a life of simple faith; of literal acceptance, of rosy dreams. We must all grant that, if it were possible, nothing would be more perfect. The highest which man can comprehend is man. One step only he may go beyond, and say that what is beyond may be different, but it cannot be less perfect than the present; the future cannot be worse than the past.

We believe in our hopes we cannot be human

enough. Let us be what we are, men, feel as men, sorrow as men, hope as men. It is true our hopes are human, but what are the doubts and difficulties? Are they not human too? Shall we meet again as we left? Maybe we do not know how it will be so, but who has a right to say it cannot be so? Let us imagine and hope for the best that, as men, we can conceive, and then rest convinced that it will be a thousand times better.

It is difficult to be always true to ourselves, to be always what we wish to be, what we feel we ought to be. As long as we feel that, as long as we do not surrender the ideal of our life, all is right. Our aspirations represent the true nature of our soul much more than our everyday life.

One sometimes forgets that all this is only the preparation for what is to come hereafter. Yet we should never forget this, otherwise this life loses its true meaning and purpose. If we only know what we live for here, we can easily find out what is worth having in this life, and what is not; we can easily go on without many things which others, whose eyes are fixed on this world only, consider essential to their happiness.

The spirit of love, and the spirit of truth, are the two life-springs of our whole being or, what is the same, of our whole religion. If we lose that bond, which holds us and binds us to a higher world, our life becomes purposeless, joyless; if it holds us and supports, life becomes perfect, all little cares vanish, and we feel we are working out a great purpose as well as we can, a purpose not our own, not selfish, not self-seeking, but, in the truest sense of the word. Gentleness is a kind of mixture of love and truthfulness, and it should be the highest object of our life to attain more and more to that true gentleness which throws such a charm over all our life. There is a gentleness of voice, of look, of movement, of speech, all of which are but the expressions of true gentleness of heart.

It is impossible to take too high a view of life; the very highest we take is still too low. One feels that more and more as our life draws to its close, and many things that seemed important once are seen to be of no consequence, while only a few things remain which will tell for ever.

How thankful we ought to be every minute of our existence.How little one has deserved this happy life, much less than many poor sufferers to whom life is a burden and a hard and bitter trial. But then, how much greater the claims on us; how much more sacred the duty never to trifle, never to waste time and power, never to compromise, but to live in all things, small and great.

How different life is to what one thought it when young, how all around us falls together, till we ourselves fall together. How meaningless and vain everything seems on earth, and how closely the reality of the life beyond approaches us.

Oh! if we could even in this life forget all that is unessential, all that makes it so hard for us to recognize true greatness and goodness in the character of those with whom this life brings us in contact for a little while! How much we lose by making little things so important, and how rarely do we think highly enough of what is essential and lasting!

The shadows fall thicker and thicker, but even in the shade it is well, often better than in full sunshine. And when the evening comes, one is tired and ready to sleep! And so all is ordered for us, if we only accommodate ourselves to it quietly.

We must take life as it is, as the way it's appointed for us, and that must lead to a certain goal. Some go sooner, some later, but we all go the same way, and all find the same place of rest. Impatience, gloom, murmurs and tears do not help us, do not alter anything, and make the road longer, not shorter. Quiet, resignation, thankfulness and faith help us forwards, and alone make it possible to perform the duties which we all, each in his own sphere, have to fulfil.

THE EFFECTS OF VISUALIZATION AND DREAMS IN OUR LIVES

Visualizations and dreams can have a strong visual element and help us to have deep, practical, solution-focus frames in complementary and practical ways. Beautiful dreams can create a bit of magic and a sense of wonder of the world.

Visualizations can act as a form of catalyst for motivation that will ultimately drive you to go above and beyond the ordinary, right up to the point of excellence.

Positive visualization helps us look at our weakness, which we can make changes to, and see results at the end of each changes that will be worth celebrating. Through visualizations we can gain experiences to realize that there is room for improvement to live accordingly with others.

When beautiful, meaningful dreams and visualization springs to our minds, we try to act upon these dreams and connect new concepts to concepts. We do this by categorizing and chaining the ideas behind each of these concepts.

Some of the most remarkable lessons in life comes from the interpretations of visualizations. Interpretations of pleasure, personal growth, how to act, how we make decisions, how we justify those decisions, how we persuade others, gives us source of knowledge, and with knowledge comes confidence, how to understand our world and act as a form of cognitive map.

I'm not saying that meaningful dreams and positive visualizations are magic solutions to every problems, but it helps heightens our awareness, challenges the human intellect, and when dreams do come through it truly touches the human heart.

Here is one of my dreams that has boosted my self confidence and helped me overcome my shyness, it is entitled. Shy guy Live Lounge Dreams.

MY LIVE LOUNGE DREAMS

There was a lady who drove a mini cooper convertible most Sunday evenings to the Live Lounge. When I heard the loud exhaust of the car, silenced by men whistling, trying to get their attention to her, I would take a detour around the bar's car park. I always like to see her stepping out of her convertible, before swishing her brunette hair around like the slow motion girl on the Loreal hair products advert.

One Sunday evening I stood outside the bar absorbing the evening breeze, the branches from the trees near the car park which stood in deep proud ranks, started dancing in the breeze. As I walked into the bar the floor surface be-lowed under my feet. A few minutes later the brunette hair lady came into the bar. I stopped and stared at her wearing a shiny necklace that sat nicely around her neck.

She caught me looking and crease her forehead. I jerked my neck as I looked away, my face as red as ripe cherries on a tree. My heart though, had leap at that sight.

Inside Live Lounge where tables of mumbling men and women, another side tables of people bellowed laughter and loud chattering. On the dance floor, tentacles of hair floated in the flashing lights, hips wriggled like jelly fish. Bright eyed girls shimmied their shiny dresses, catching the disco light like silver darlings. A stern face man standing next to me was tapping his fingers on the bar counter with an insistent rhythm.

I looked up and a lady smiled at me, I glanced behind me in case it had been a mistake, I almost trip over, other girls in the bar giggled, their kaleidoscopic faces drew me to them like bubbles to the surface.

The sounds of music playing and people chatting drowned out their gossips as they cupped hands over ears. I hit the dance floor and started some of the latest dance moves you could think of. Suddenly a circle of people gathered around me one of them pointed at my snake skin shoe which matched with the rest of my clothing. I couldn't careless if they were taking the mickey. Then the crowed got larger gathering round to see my dance moves.

Ryan was standing among them, he was jabbing at the shoulder of one of the guys in the circle trying to copy my dance moves. But a lady moved straight towards me. I looked at her a little sweat began to trickled down my forehead. She started talking to me, she was so close I could smell the perfume she was wearing. It was the brunette who drove the mini cooper convertible. She stretched her arm towards me and we started dancing.

The music had softened, the frantic disco lights faded and I thought that was it. As I was about to break away another song started up. We danced again. I peep around the dance floor bodies where bouncing in delight. I caught the shape of a white shirt skulking on a stool that aches your bum in half an hour. There he was, it was Adam, leaning forward, elbows on his thighs, a knuckled hand griped a bottle of budwiser wedged to his mouth. I turned away quickly to stare into the angel eyes of the mini cooper lady.

After the final song I head off home. I snuggled under the warm covers to sleep. The next morning I woke up the mini cooper lady was outside my house. Her eyes glittered in the morning light. "Hello you" she said. "Morning I didn't catch your name." "Jody your dancing partner last night." "The dance was god eh?" I mustered to her. She beamed at me, and a population of butterflies had a party in my stomach.

I looked straight into her eyes, her smile was like an invisible force drawing me to her, I was putty but she couldn't resist hugging me, we both giggled as we hugged, it felt like she hugged me over a hundred times. I checked that I wasn't in my night gear and this magical feeling wasn't a dream. I let out a sigh and woke up, it was a dream.

DE-CLUTTER OUR BRAIN FROM A STRESSFUL LIFE

We tend to live stressful lives and rarely have spare time for ourselves. The stress can lead to anxiety, which leads to more stress.

A technique I would like to introduce to you is the writing of morning pages. Morning pages declutters the worries in your brain, gets you calmer and smarter. It will at times leave you feeling extra ordinary unique as a special being. Its truly a remedy for a stressful life.

How can you find time in writing one or two pages into this day, that is packed with so much things to do with our daily living activities? You don't have to be a writer to start writing morning pages. Just write anything that comes to your mind without judging your writing. You might be going through guilt, suffering, emotional pain, joy, past jokes that put a smile on your face.

WRITING MORNING PAGES TECHNIQUE
Here is a brief demonstration of how you could write a morning page.

Early this morning, I was awakened by the crowing of a cockerel on my alarm clock. I stretched and cracked in my fingers with a restless yarn, showered and brush my teeth. I then sat on my comfortable cough sipping a nice cup of herbal tea, my body fill with energy I decide to write down a list of things I am presently grateful for and things I'd like to get done for this day.

Things I'm grateful for which read like this;

o   My mind – For the ability to think and write these morning pages.
o   Life – For Facing a new day
o   Happiness – For me to soak in this beauty of been optimistic
o   Sunrise – For bringing light and radiance around us
o   Knowledge – To add wisdom to our lives

Morning pages: Today I need to arrive at class at 09.00am for a 09.30am start, I need to remain focus, calm, relax during my exam. Today I need to be optimistic that I will get a good grade in my exam. Today I need to bin feeling nervous. Today I need a healthy breakfast, not too heavy. Today I need to have a good body scrub before I face the public. Today I need to read exam questions and instructions carefully to avoid making simple mistakes. Today I will wear my lucky shirt, it has always given me good luck in the past. Today after exam I will play a few games of pool to socialize and unwind with friends. This afternoon I will listen to a genre of music. This evening I need to treat myself to a nice dessert as a form of reward for completing the exams. This evening I need to learn a new skill e.g. making cocktails, even if they don't taste nice. This evening I need to say hello to my neighbor as we haven't talk for a couple of days. Tonight I would like to watch a champions league football game.

BENEFITS OF WRITING MORNING PAGES

o Motivational status. For example, what you actually want to do about your day and when.
o You will be able to work out issues that were bothering you.
o Brings serenity and quietened your over active mind.
o Assist you as a tool for personal life growth.
o Helps you get on with life challenges in a positive, optimistic way by taken constructive actions.
o Helps you develop a self awareness of the hear and now.
o Helps you practice good time management.
o Gives you the capacity to think critically and creatively.

LETTING GO

Today is a new day. Today is a day you can begin, creating a joyous, fulfilling day. Today is a day to write a new chapter in your life, the most beautiful chapter.

It is best to live in the present times. If you keep looking back to see what is in the rear view mirror you will find it difficult to move on.

It can get tiring holding on to negative emotions and blaming others for our problems, poverty, and poor relationships. Remember you're not a bad person for thinking the way you do. However, blaming others will ultimately lead us into a trap and allow everything and everyone around us to dictate our lives.

Some people who want to move on in life are hindered through no fault of their own, I define life as a challenge all human being must face. Some people's challenges are much harder than others.

You can change your life, you've already got the tools to do so. Some of these tools are your thoughts and beliefs. You are the undisputed champion of yourself, the architect of your life.

Our lives are like cameras so:

o Focus
o Capture
o Develop

Try new positive things and if things don't workout, take another shot. When one door is closed others are open. Hold on to love, intimacy, passion, honesty, feelings, commitment, truth, and authenticity. Use your will power, your strong mind and your other natural abilities to realize your purpose in life. Living a rich, full, meaningful life is not an easy journey as I've already discovered. However, its a journey worth taking.

Your life living is your own personal quest not others.

SEARCHING FOR A PURPOSEFUL LIFE AS AN INDIVIDUAL

JULIA STORY

My name is Julia my parents met when they where teenagers and got married a few years later.

They planned two children, my brother and I. We had a very good childhood both of my parents worked they were never on benefits. We had, family holidays' each year. We never had much but we where contended wit what we have, so I have good memories of my childhood.

Moving into my teenage days, I tried to push the boundaries with my parents, by being rebellious and spending lots of time in the pub. Then I meet my first boyfriend and he was in a popular group of lads, so everyone in the neighborhood knew him, we had lots of fun and I fell pregnant in my late teens.

I was working full-time in hairdressing and my wage would go on baby stuff. I left work as my boss did not want an unmarried teenage mum working for her.

When my baby reached a year old. I tried to find employment as an hairdresser again. They all turn me down, and I realize I was now a single has my first boyfriend and I split.

I spent the next sixteen months figuring out what to do. I got various menial jobs in the area. I met my second boyfriend then I moved out of my parents house and lived with my second boyfriend. I continued to work partime and had my second child, just after my first started school. Once again I was out of work, I left my second partner. I started to work partime again. Things stayed the same for a little while until my second child started going school.

I went back to college full-time and that's when I got the qualification I should have got when I was at school.

Suddenly I realize that I wasn't achieving much, when I reached my late twenties, I started to strive for a purposeful life. The college qualifications gave me the skills I needed to set up my own business. I negotiated a deal with trust organization and got a small fund to help with the business start up.

Things got better, the business started booming, I was turning over a lot of money and became very comfortable financially. I was putting in lots of hours and the job was very satisfactory. My children where benefiting, they had really wonderful Christmas, holidays' abroad, and I spent quality time with them. Teaching them, basically how to do household chores and life skills.

I bought a house, everything was looking up. Then I met my third partner and two and a half years later we decided to live together, and that's when things started to take a turn for the worse. He had a good job, but he had a problem with self-esteem and security because of that I made a lot of compromises in terms of getting joint bank accounts, and the things we did on a day to day basis.

About a year later in our relationship I lost my dad it was very sudden and unexpected. My partner at the time supported me. However, this is where he started to show is true colors. He started to lie a lot about pointless things, he was spending more than he was telling me, which got us into debts. I would always bail him out with my money and he would continue to do it again. It became obvious that he had a drinking problem . He then became an aggressive person towards me. He continued to drink irresponsible and secretly as I wasn't aware of it at the time. It was only when he started having health issues that I realize it was the drink that made him become so aggressive and that was the reason we got into debts.

After the second time he was admitted into hospital, he stopped the drinking for a good few months, he became less moody, loss weight, his eyes cleared up, and he stopped spending unnecessary which made a better atmosphere at home for a short period.

He started drinking again, because he thought he could handle it but he couldn't, so all the hard work he did over the last few months had gone to waste. We started arguing and the little manipulation and control became obvious to me. I told him if things didn't change I would leave him. It got worse and the final straw was when he set fire to the house, he got arrested. I left him that very day.

In the few months after I received a notification from a company recovering debt in my name for items I never had or new nothing about.

Upon investigation I discovered, he had committed fraud by using my name to purchase items that he had no intentions of paying for. That was one of the lowest points has I felt so betrayed, and also I actually had to closed down my business as everything I sacrificed just to be with him. It felt like a big kick in my face, I was really at rock bottom.

I started to think now I've got to start over again. I decided to go back to college and equipped myself with the skills to go into the beautician industry, with a view to start up another business.

I worked in an office par-time whilst, doing my training at college. Once I qualified it was time for me to start making plans to set up a business.

I started to think how I could make the business successful. But I faced a critical point where I needed to make a decision whether to leave my office job with a regularly salary and invest into a new business so quickly.

I'm at the point of my life now, hoping the decision to start up this new business is going to pay off.

KELLY STORY

My name is Kelly. I'm the eldest of three children. I had a very challenging childhood as I had to grow up very quickly cause it was my duty to care for my siblings.

My father was in the army and my mother worked full-time, seven days a week. Up to the age of eleven brings back some happy memories. Lots of family activities which includes home baking, holidays', dressing up, swimming, bike-riding.

My dad came out of the army and we fell on hard times, which meant my mum had to continue working seven days per week and more responsibilities for me such as . Cooking evening meals and picking up my younger siblings from school. Family activities became far and few in between, and I sometimes felt alienated. Hence I started to resent my own sisters.

I began to act out just to receive some attention. I found it difficult to make or trust friends, as I put up a barrier. I immersed myself into books.

In my late teens I started to make bad choices such as hanging around bad people a lot older than myself, visiting pub gigs on a regular basis as an escape route, has I felt like there was no one I could talk to who would truly understand what it feels like to be me.

One day I had a massive row with my parents, hence I moved out and link up with my aunt who told me to stay at hers. I met a male friend much older than I was, who happen to live across the road from my aunt. I thought it was really exciting that someone really liked me for who I was.

One evening we where out on his motorbike and we where involved in an accident. I quickly realize after that accident who my true friends and family were, I also realized that I needed to go back home to live with my parents.

The family sat down and I told them what happened, and how I've been feeling about their resentment towards me at such a young age.

My parents were mortified and felt like failures that they let me down and not been able to protect me. Eventually things got a bit better, I got back into school work and did extremely well, but still had that wall of not trusting others. I somehow let my guard down and became friends with someone whom I thought was special, only to be let down. And I had a nervous breakdown, but recovered from that a year later.

I want to care for people in ways that I wasn't care for. So I decide to become a nurse and I got a job in a hospital. That was when I meet my husband. I was very career focused and put a lot of energy into my work. My husband and I started trying for a baby, but I was told I could not have children which was devastating. Against all odds few months after I became pregnant and I gave up my nursing job as I wanted to be a full time mum. I didn't want my child t grow up with the same experience as I did.

Five years later we had our second child. However when she was two I had to get back into work. I got a job offer in a different city. My husband and I decided we would move, as it was a very good job offer at an hospital.

My mum got seriously ill and was diagnosed with cancer, all the treatments failed and they gave her eight weeks to live. I made the decision that my mum would not die in hospital, so I brought her home to be with my family. She passed away four months later. They were the best and precious months of my life with my mother.

She made me realize life is too short to hold on to negative emotions and not follow your dreams, I also realized that she did truly loved me.

I made a decision that no matter what life challenges and sufferings we all face. I will always follow my positive dreams.

DAVE STORY

I was born on the first of January, new years day, which was the same birthday as my mum. So every year was a competition of who would received the most birthday cards and presents. Being born on new years day like my mum, meant we had a very close bond.

I had a good childhood, with good parents who cared for me, the best way they could. My mum and dad where married before they got together, in which they had a child from their first marriage. When they got together they had me and my younger brother.

Growing up and going to school was very enjoyable from the age of nine I was well into my sports, football was the main sport I enjoyed.

I played for a team called Alton United, which my dad was the manager of. We started off been a crap team, but each year we played, we kept getting better, we end up been runners up of the division.

At age thirteen I found out, I got diabetes, I found it hard to take in. From being a happy go lucky teenager, to start taking several injections a day to keep me alive. It was hard for me to keep going to the doctors on a regular basis as I like my sports.

A couple of years after, some new people moved next door me and my family. My new neighbors children where the same age group as me. I started to hang about with them and started getting into trouble, bunking school and getting suspended. I stopped playing football because of this.

When I finished school I went to college, I wanted to do an electrician course, there wasn't enough students on that course, so I did construction course instead. I got a part time job working at Sainsbury's for two years whilst I did my studying at college. Until my dad asked me to come and work for him at his builders merchant and construction company.

Shortly after my mum died from cancer this was a very hard time for me as I was close to my mum. I loved her with every strand of my being.

Everyone copes with their grief journey differently. I didn't go back to work for two months after my mum's death. Has I felt unmotivated.

However, luckily for me I had a closely knit team of friends and families, partly by helping me make significant small steps towards recovery. They were so attentive during this time. I really had to question my meaningless existence.

Now there's been quite a shift in values. These values has caused me to be more contended and to contribute more to my fathers construction company for a continued success. And keep feeling a fulfill life purpose.

JAKE STORY

From a very young age my life was traumatic. Both my parents where in the serving in the army and my school days was dysfunctional, as I endured a lot of bullying from my school peers.

To escape the bullying my grandmother sent me to a dancing drama centre, and I thrived, made lots of life long friends.

I really enjoyed performing at the grand theatre and through it I ended up performing a major bally company. It also opened up lots of doors and opportunities and my confidence soared.

During my late teen years I built my resilience got my GCSE O and A Level's and went on to university and gained a honorary degree.

After graduation I immediately got taken on in the profession of acting and was on tour for several years doing television work. However, the roles that I was assigned to dried up, and the hours of work wasn't suitable enough.

I decided to try and rebuild a genuine relationship with my mother and siblings which I found difficult to start with, compromising on both sides. Things gradually got better and after a period of time, things are now good between myself and my family.

It wasn't my wish to stay at home without a job. Hence I got a job as a despatch manager for a brewing company.

I meet a friend whom I had a beautiful son with, and she did not let me see him for over twenty years. It made me question human nature.

I wished I had a better relationship with my father, and it made me feel sad about the relationship I have with my son. I'm trying my best to make up for the lost years with my son, which will make us both happy.

Whilst working for the brewer's company my long term partner whom I spend many happy years with, decided to go our separate ways has things changed massively for worse.

Thankfully through my faith it made me realize people can be selfish, but we nee to understand their reasons, and not keep hanging on to the hurt, slowly the hurt and anger that was in me evaporated.

Few years after something horrible happened that dramatically changed my life, I lost my grandmother who brought me up, and she was my favorite friend.

Several months after another close family member passed away, and not since my grandmother passed away I felt such hurt. He died in my arms looking into my eyes. It was this experience that made me question the purpose of life and how I can developed a sense of this world.

LIVING A HAPPY AND PURPOSEFUL LIFE

LIVING A HAPPY AND PURPOSEFUL LIFE

We can experience a happy and purposeful life through.

o Employment
o Adequate food, shelter, clean air, water,clothing
o Grattitudes
o Good health
o Peace and security
o Love/kindness
o Using our talents/wisdom
o Loving family and friends
o Meditations

These experiences for living a happy and purposeful life may sound simple. But for many people, some or all these experiences are hard to meet.

LOVING FAMILY, AND RELATIONSHIPS

WHAT WE COULD DO TO MAINTAIN GOOD FAMILY RELATIONSHIPS

Respect: Respectful families and friends care about each other even during disagreement. Instead they listen respectfully to another perspectives, and they find compromises that work for both sides.

Without respect, conversations between friends can become laced with criticism, sarcasm, and even contempt.

Learn to forgive: To forgive means that you let go of an offense any feelings of resentment it may have caused. Forgiveness does not require that you minimize the wrong or pretend it never occurred.

If you hold on to resentment, you can harm yourself physically and emotionally. You can also damage the relationships bond.

Good communication: Genuine communication takes place when you and your families, friends partners share a two-way exchange of thoughts and feelings.

Communications is the bridge that keeps you connected with each other.

Values: Values are the personal standards by which you choose to live. Values also include ethical standards. For example, a person with solid ethics is industrious, fair, and considerate of others, traits that are best developed while a person is still young.

Identity: Your identity goes far beyond your name and appearance. It involves your values, beliefs, and character. Really, your identity is everything that makes you, both inside and out.

When you have a strong sense of identity, you stand up for your beliefs instead of allowing your peers to control you

Trustworthiness: Trustworthy people earn the confidence of their parents, friends, and employers. They abide by the rules, keep their promises, and always tell the truth

In most cases, the amount of freedom you receive is directly related to the level of trust you have earned over time.

Industriousness: Industrious people do not shy away from work rather, they enjoy working hard to provide for their personal needs and to help others, even if the work they do is not glamorous.

Like it or not, life is full of responsibilities. When you work hard, you get a sense of pride and inner satisfaction.

Goals: A goal is more than just a dream, something you wish would happen. Real goals involve planning, flexibility, and hard work.

Goal can be short-range, medium-range, long-range. Reaching goals can boost your confidence, strengthen your friendships, and increase your happiness. Goals are also like blue prints; with effort, you can turn them into reality.

Affection: Its the atmosphere that should pervade the household. "Without hearts," it has been truly said, "there is no home." A collection of roots, and trunk, and branches, and leaves, do not make a tree; neither do a number of people dwelling together make a home. "A certain number of animal lives that are of prescribed ages, that eat and drink together, by no means makes a family. Almost as well might we say that it is the bricks of a house that make a home. There may be a home in the forest or in the wilderness, and there may be a family with all its blessings, though half its members be in other lands or in another world. It is the gentle memories, the mutual thought, the desire to bless, the sympathies that meet when duties are apart, the fervor of the parents' prayers, the persuasion of filial love, the sister's pride and the brother's benediction, that constitute the true elements of domestic life and sanctify the dwelling." A home without love is no home, any more than a body without a soul is a man.

Consideration: For those with whom we live in the family is the chief form which affection takes. Each member has to remember, not his own comfort and wants, but the comfort and wants of those with whom he dwells. His welfare as an individual he must subordinate to the welfare of the household. There are various forms which want of consideration takes, and all of them are detestable. (a) Tyranny, where the strong member of a family insists on the service of those weaker than himself. (b) Greed, where one demands a larger share of comfort, food, or attention than that which falls to the others. (c) Indolence, where one refuses to take his proper part in the maintenance of the family, spending his wages, perhaps, on his own pleasures, and yet expecting to be provided for by the labor of the rest. (d) Discourtesy, where, by his language and manners, he makes the others unhappy, and, perhaps, by his outbursts of temper fills the whole house with sadness. (e) Obstinacy, which will have its own way, whether the way be good or not. All these forms of selfishness are violations of the true law of family life, and render that life impossible. In the family, more than in any other sphere, everyone should bear the burdens of others. Everyone should seek, not his own, but another's welfare, and the weak and feeble should receive the attention of all.

Pleasantness: Should be the disposition which we should specially cultivate at home. If we have to encounter things that annoy and perhaps irritate us in the outer world, we should seek to leave the irritation and annoyance behind when we cross the threshold of our dwelling. Into it the roughness and bluster of the world should never be permitted to come. It should be the place of "sweetness and light," and every member may do something to make it so. It is a bad sign when a young man never cares to spend his evenings at home, when he prefers the company of others to the society of his family, and seeks his amusement wholly beyond its circle. A young man, it is admitted, may find his home uninviting through causes for which he has not himself to blame. Still, even then he may do much to change its character, and by his pleasant and cheerful bearing may bring into it sunshine brighter than the sunshine outside.

HAPPINESS

Happiness has been described as a state of well-being that is characterized by relative permanence, by emotions ranging from mere contentment to deep and intense joy in living, and by a natural desire for it to continue.

Happiness results from following a good path in life, living in harmony with good principles. Many people experience a measure of happiness when they achieve a certain goal or obtain a desired item.

How long that surge of happiness last? It is usually temporary which can be disappointing.

I believe that human's are born with the natural ability to be happy, and that being happy is simple. Being unhappy is complicated.

So then what makes you happy? Your family, close friend, music, comedies, sex, chocolates, good physical health, bunch of flowers, Christmas gifts, the list goes on.

Perhaps you are looking forward to something that may make you happy. Things like, getting married, birthdays, going for a nice meal with your partner, receiving roses, graduating, buying a car, a house, going on nice holidays'.

Happiness comes to those who:

o Are content with what they have
o Build resilience
o View life as sacred
o Focus on positive thoughts
o Love, respect and keep genuine friends
o Utilizes love to make it become essential to their mental health.
o Have healthy relationships and inner peace

AN OVERVIEW OF HAPPINESS

The psychological and philosophical pursuit of happiness began in China, India, and Greece some 2,500 years ago with Confucius, Buddha,Socrates, and Aristotle.

SOCRATES

Socrates has a unique place in the history of happiness, as he is the first known figure in the west to argue that happiness is actually obtainable through human effort.

Like most ancient peoples, the Greeks had a pessimistic view of human existence. Happiness was deemed a rare occurrence and reserved only for those whom the gods favored. The idea that one could obtain happiness for oneself was considered "hubris", a kind of over-reaching pride and was met with harsh punishment.

The optimistic Socrates enters the picture. The key to happiness, he argues, is to turn attention away from the body and towards the soul. By harmonizing our desires we can learn to pacify the mind and achieve a divine-like state of tranquility. A moral life is to be preferred to an immoral one, primarily because it leads to a happier life.

We see right here at the beginning of western philosophy that happiness is at the forefront, linked to other concepts such as virtue, justice, and the ultimate meaning of existence.

Socrates was very interested in ethical and social issues such as. What is the best way to live? Why be moral when immoral people seem to benefit more? Is happiness satisfying one's desires or is it virtuous activity?

Famously, Socrates was more adept at asking such questions than spoon-feeding us the answers. His "Socratic method" consisted of a process of questioning designed to expose ignorance and clear the way for knowledge. Socrates himself admits that he is ignorant, and yet he became one of the wisest men through his self-knowledge.

The price Socrates paid for his honest truth was death. He was convicted of "corrupting the youth" and sentenced to die by way of hen-lock poisoning.

As long as there is a mind that earnestly seeks to explore and understand the world, there will be opportunities to expand one's consciousness and achieve an increasingly happier mental state. Through is influence on Plato and Aristotle, a new era of philosophy was inaugurated and the course of western civilization was decisively shaped.

Although Socrates didn't write anything himself, his student Plato wrote a voluminous number of dialogues with him as the central character. Scholarly debate still rages as to the relationship between Socrates original teachings and Plato's own evolving ideas.

Some of Socrates quotes:

o "An unexamined life is not worth living"
o "True knowledge exists in knowing that you know nothing"
o "Wisdom begins in wonder"
o True wisdom comes to each of us when we realize how little we understand about life, ourselves and the world around us
o He who is not contended with what he has, would not be contended with what he would like to have
o Falling down is not a failure. Failure comes when you stay where you have fallen

BUDDHA

For Buddha, the path to happiness starts from understanding of the root causes of suffering. Those who consider Buddha a pessimist because of his concern with suffering have missed the point. In fact, he his a skillful doctor, he may break the bad news of our suffering, but he also prescribes a proactive course of treatment.

During the late 6th and early 5th centuries BCE, Siddhartha Gautama of Shakya, who later became known as Buddha was born in modern-day Nepal near the Indian border. While there are mythical stories surrounding his conception and birth, the basic facts of his life are generally agreed upon.

Born into a wealthy royal family, the Buddha was born and raised in worldly luxury. Despite his father's attempt to shield him from the ugliness of life. One day he ventured out beyond the castle walls and encountered three aspects of life: the old, the sick, and the dead. Each of these experiences troubled him and made him question the meaning and transience of life and its pleasures.

After this, he encountered an ascetic who, by

choice, lived a life renouncing the pleasures of the world. Even while he was completely deprived of life's comforts, his eyes shined with contentment. These shocking experiences moved Buddha to renounce his comfortable lifestyle in search of greater meaning in life. It was during his time practicing extreme forms of self-denial that Buddha discovered the "Middle path" of moderation, an idea that closely resembles Aristotle's "Golden mean"

During his life, he had experienced intensive pleasure and extreme deprivation but he found that neither extreme brought one to true understanding. He then practiced meditation through deep concentration (Dhyana) under a bondi tree and found enlightenment. He began teaching the four noble truths to others in order to help them achieve transcendent happiness and peace of mind through the knowledge and practice known today as Buddhism.

THE FOUR NOBLE TRUTHS AND THE EIGHT-FOLD PATH TO HAPPINESS

Buddha taught his followers the Four Noble Truths as follows:

1. Life is/means Dukkha (mental dysfunction or suffering)
2. Dukkha arises from craving

3. Dukkha can be eliminated
4. The way to the elimination of Dukkha is the Eight-Fold Path

THE EIGHT-FOLD PATH

The Eight-Fold Path is often divided into the three categories of wisdom (right view/ understanding, right intention), ethical conduct (right speech, right action, right livelihood and mental cultivation (right effort, right mindfulness, right concentration)

Right view/understanding	Wisdom
Right intention/thought	Wisdom
Right speech	Ethical Conduct
Right action	Ethical Conduct
Right livelihood	Ethical Conduct
Right Effort	Mental Cultivation
Right Mindfulness	Mental Cultivation
Right Concentration	Mental Cultivation

The Eight-fold Path is a practical and systematic way out of ignorance, eliminating Dukkha from our minds and our lifestyle through mindful thoughts and actions. It is presented as a whole system, but the three paths associated with the area of mental cultivation are particularly relevant to the happiness that we can find in equanimity, or peace of mind.

BUDDHA

Buddhism pursues happiness by using knowledge and practice to achieve mental equanimity. In Buddhism, equanimity, or peace of mind, is achieved by detaching oneself from the cycle of craving that produces Dukkha. So by achieving a mental state where you can detached from all the passions, needs and wants of life, you free yourself and achieve a state of transcendent bliss and well-being.

MINDFULNESS

Mindfulness is one of the most influential teachings of Buddhism and has filtered into popular culture as well as psychotherapy. The Buddha felt that it was imperative to cultivate right mindfulness for all aspects of life in order to see things as they really are, or in other words, to "stop and smell the roses." He encouraged keen attention and awareness of all things through the four foundations of mindfulness.

o Contemplation of the body
o Contemplation of feelings
o Contemplation of states of mind
o Contemplation of phenomena

Stories of Buddha compassion and consideration for all life bound. He taught truth and also taught compassion because he saw personal happiness as related to happiness for others, humans and otherwise. Such a lesson is reflected in both the way he lived and the way he died.

SOME BUDDHA QUOTES

o Health is the greatest gift, contentment the greatest wealth, faithfulness the best relationship.

o Holding on to anger is like grasping a hot coal with the intent of throwing it at someone else; you are the one who gets burned

o You, yourself, as much as anybody in the entire universe, deserve your love and affection

ARISTOTLE

Aristotle is one of the greatest thinkers in history of western science and philosophy, making contributions to logic, metaphysics, mathematics, physics, biology, botany, ethics, politics, agriculture, medicine, dance and theatre. He was a student of Plato who in turn studied under Socrates.

Aristotle define happiness in four simple words "happiness depends on ourselves. More than anybody else, Aristotle shrines happiness as a central purpose of human life and a goal in itself. As a result he devotes more space to the topic of happiness than any thinker prior to modern era.

Living during the same period as Meniscus, but, on the other side of the world, he draws some similar conclusion. That happiness depends on cultivation of virtue, though his virtues are somewhat more individualistic than the essentially social virtues of the Confucians.

Aristotle was convinced that a genuinely happy life required the fulfillment of a broad range of conditions, including physical as well as mental well-being. In this way he introduced the idea of a "science of happiness" in the classical sense, in terms of a new field of knowledge.

Aristotle was the first to classify areas of human knowledge into distinct disciplines such as mathematics, biology and ethics. Some of these classifications are still used today, such as the species-genus system taught in biology classes. He was the first to devise a formal system for reasoning, whereby the validity of an argument is determined by its structure rather than its content.

Aristotle was the founder of the Lyceum, the first scientific institute, based in Athens Greece. Along with his teacher Plato, he was one of the strongest advocates of liberal arts education, which stresses the education of the whole person, including one's moral character, rather than merely learning a set of skills. According to Aristotle, this view of education is necessary if we are to produce a society of happy as well as productive individuals.

One of Aristotle's most influential works is the Nicomachean ethics, where he presents a theory of happiness that is still relevant today. The key question Aristotle seeks to answer in these lectures is "What is the ultimate purpose of human existence?" What is that end or goal for which we see people seeking pleasure, wealth, and a good reputation?" But while each of these has some value, none of them can occupy the place of the chief good for which humanity should aim.

Aristotle would be strongly critical of the culture of "instant gratification" which seems to predominate in our society today. In order to achieve the life of complete virtue, we need to make the right choices, and this involves keeping our eye on the future, on the ultimate result we want for our lives as a whole. We will not achieve happiness simply by enjoying the pleasures of the moment. Unfortunately, this is something most people are not able to overcome in themselves.

According to Aristotle, what is happiness?

o Happiness is the ultimate end and purpose of human existence.

o Happiness is not pleasure, nor is it virtue. It is the exercise of virtue.

o Happiness cannot be achieved until the end of one's life. Hence it is a goal and not a temporary state.

o Happiness is the perfection of human nature. Since man is a rational animal, human happiness depends on the exercise of his reason.

o Happiness depends on acquiring a moral character, where one displays these virtues of courage, generosity, justice, friendship, and citizenship in one's life. These virtues involve striking a balance or "mean" between an excess and a deficiency.

o Happiness requires intellectual contemplation, for this is the ultimate realization of our rational capacities.

o Happiness is a journey not a destination.

SOME QUOTES OF ARISTOTLE

o Man is a goal seeking animal. His life only has meaning if he's reaching out and striving for his goals.

o Through discipline comes freedom

o A friend to all is a friend to none

o All human actions have one or more of these causes: Chance, nature, compulsion, habit, reason, passion, desire

DEVELOPING A HAPPY OUTLOOK

Happiness is not a simple goal, but is about making progress, when it's as elusive as ever. Being happy often means continually finding satisfaction, contentment, a feeling of joy, and a sense that your life is meaningful during all kinds of problems, that does not depend upon finding ease or comfort. Nobody is jolly or elated all the time, but some individuals are definitely more fulfilled/fortunate than others.

Happiness is the greatest paradox in Nature. It can grow in any soil, live under any conditions. It defies environment. It comes from within; it is the revelation of the depths of the inner life as light and heat proclaim the sun from which they radiate. Happiness consists not of having, but of being; not of possessing, but of enjoying. It is the warm glow of a heart at peace with itself. A martyr at the stake may have happiness that a king on his throne might envy. Man is the creator of his own happiness; it is the aroma of a life lived in harmony with high ideals. For what a man has, he may be dependent on others; what he is, rests with him alone. What he obtains

GOLDEN PURPOSES OF LIFE

in life is but acquisition; what he attains, is growth. Happiness is the soul's joy in the possession of the intangible. Absolute, perfect, continuous happiness in life, is impossible for the human. It would mean the consummation of attainments, the individual consciousness of a perfectly fulfilled destiny. Happiness is paradox because it may coexist with trial, sorrow and poverty. It is the gladness of the heart, rising superior to all conditions.

Happiness has a number of under-studies, gratification, satisfaction, content, and pleasure, clever imitators that simulate its appearance rather than emulate its method. Gratification is a harmony between our desires and our possessions. It is ever incomplete, it is the thankful acceptance of part. It is a mental pleasure in the quality of what one receives, an unsatisfying as to the quantity. It may be an element in happiness, but, in itself, it is not happiness.

Satisfaction is perfect identity of our desires and our possessions. It exists only so long as this perfect union and unity can be preserved. But every realized ideal gives birth to new ideals, every step in advance reveals large domains of the unattained; every feeding stimulates new appetites, – then the desires and possessions are no longer identical, no longer equal; new cravings call forth new activities, the equipoise is destroyed, and dissatisfaction reenters. Man might possess everything tangible in the world and yet not be happy, for happiness is the satisfying of the soul, not of the mind or the body. Dissatisfaction, in its highest sense, is the keynote of all advance, the evidence of new aspirations, the guarantee of the progressive revelation of new possibilities.

Happiness represents a peaceful attunement of a life with a standard of living. It can never be made by the individual, by himself, for himself. It is one of the incidental by-products of an unselfish life. No man can make his own happiness the one object of his life and attain it, any more than he can jump on the far end of his shadow. If you would hit the bull's-eye of happiness on the target of life, aim above it. Place other things higher than your own happiness and it will surely come to you. You can buy pleasure, you can acquire content, you can become satisfied, – but Nature never put real happiness on the bargain-counter. It is the undetachable accompaniment of true living. It is calm and peaceful; it never lives in an atmosphere of worry or of hopeless struggle.

The basis of happiness is the love of something outside self. Search every instance of happiness in the world, and you will find, when all the incidental features are eliminated, there is always the constant, unchangeable element of love, – love of parent for child; love of man and woman for each other; love of humanity in some form, or a great life work into which the individual throws all his energies.

Happiness is the voice of optimism, of faith, of simple, steadfast love. No cynic or pessimist can be really happy. A cynic is a man who is morally near-sighted, and brags about it. He sees the evil in his own heart, and thinks he sees the world. He lets a mote in his eye eclipse the sun. An incurable cynic is an individual who should long for death, for life cannot bring him happiness, death might. The keynote of Bismarck's lack of happiness was his profound distrust of human nature. There is a royal road to happiness; it lies in Consecration, Concentration, Conquest and Conscience.

Consecration is dedicating the individual life to the service of others, to some noble mission, to realizing some unselfish ideal. Life is not something to be lived through; it is something to be lived up to. It is a privilege, not a penal servitude of so many decades on earth. Consecration places the object of life above the mere acquisition of money, as a finality. The man who is unselfish, kind, loving, tender, helpful, ready to lighten the burden of those around him, to hearten the struggling ones, to forget himself sometimes in remembering others, is on the right road to happiness. Consecration is ever active, bold and aggressive, fearing naught but possible disloyalty to high ideals.

Concentration makes the individual life simpler and deeper. It cuts away the shams and pretenses of modern living and limits life to its truest essentials. Worry, fear, useless regret, all the great wastes that sap mental, moral or physical energy must be sacrificed, or the individual needlessly destroys half the possibilities of living. A great purpose in life, something that unifies the strands and threads of each day's thinking, something that takes the sting from the petty trials, sorrows, sufferings and blunders of life, is a great aid to concentration. Soldiers in battle may forget their wounds, or even be unconscious of them, in the inspiration of battling for what they believe is right. Concentration dignifies an humble life; it makes a great life, sublime. In morals it is a short-cut to simplicity. It leads to right for right's sake, without thought of policy or of reward. It brings calm and rest to the individual, a serenity that is but the sunlight of happiness.

Conquest is the overcoming of an evil habit, the rising superior to opposition and attack, the spiritual exaltation that comes from resisting the invasion of the grovelling material side of life. Sometimes when you are worn and weak with the struggle; when it seems that justice is a dream, that honesty and loyalty and truth count for nothing, that the devil is the only good paymaster; when hope grows dim and flickers, then is the time when you must tower in the great sublime faith that Right must prevail, then must you throttle these imps of doubt and despair, you must master yourself to master the world around you. This is conquest; this is what counts. Even a log can float with the current, it takes a man to fight sturdily against an opposing tide that would sweep his craft out of its course. When the jealousies, the petty intrigues and the meanness's and the misunderstandings in life assail you, rise above them. Be like a lighthouse that illumines and beautifies the snarling, swashing waves of the storm that threaten it, that seek to undermine it and seek to wash over it. This is conquest. When the chance to win fame, wealth, success or the attainment of your heart's desire, by sacrifice of honor or principle, comes to you and it does not affect you long enough even to seem a temptation, you have been the victor. That too is conquest. And conquest is part of the royal road to Happiness.

Conscience, as the mentor, the guide and compass of every act, leads ever to Happiness. When the individual can stay alone with his conscience and get its approval, without using force or specious logic, then he begins to know what real Happiness is. But the individual must be careful that he is not appealing to a conscience perverted or deadened by the wrongdoing and subsequent deafness of its owner. The man who is honestly seeking to live his life in consecration, concentration and conquest, living from day to day as best he can, by the light he has, may rely explicitly on his conscience. He can shut his ears to "what the world says" and find in the approval of his own conscience the highest earthly tribune, the voice of the Infinite communing with the Individual.

Unhappiness is the hunger to get; Happiness is the hunger to give. True happiness must ever have the tinge of sorrow outlived, the sense of pain softened by the mellowing years, the chastening of loss that in the wondrous mystery of time transmutes our suffering into love and sympathy with others.

If the individual should set out for a single day to give Happiness, to make life happier, brighter and sweeter, not for himself, but for others, he would find a wondrous revelation of what Happiness really is. The greatest of the world's heroes could not by any series of acts of heroism do as much real good as any individual living his whole life in seeking, from day to day, to make others happy.

Each day there should be fresh resolution, new strength, and renewed enthusiasm. "Just for Today" might be the daily motto of thousands of societies throughout the continents, composed of members bound together to make the world better through constant simple acts of kindness, constant deeds of sweetness and love. And Happiness would come to them, in its highest and best form, not because they would seek to absorb it, but, because they seek to radiate it.

CHANGING TIMES

The world looks like a multiplication table, or a mathematical equation, which, turn it how you will, balances itself. Take what figure you will, its exact value, nor more nor less, still returns to you. Every secret is told, every crime is punished, every virtue rewarded, every wrong redressed, in silence and certainty. What we call retribution is the universal necessity by which the whole appears wherever a part appears. If you see smoke, there must be fire. If you see a hand or limb, you know that the trunk to which it belongs is there behind.

Such, also, is the natural history of calamity. The changes which break up at short intervals the prosperity of men are advertisements of a nature whose law is growth. Every soul is by this intrinsic necessity quitting its whole system of things, its friends, and home, and laws, and faith, as the shellfish crawls out of its beautiful but stony case, because it no longer admits of its growth, and slowly forms a new house. In proportion to the vigor of the individual, these revolutions are frequent, until in some happier mind they are incessant, and all worldly relations hang very loosely about him, becoming, as it were, a transparent fluid membrane through which the living form is seen, and not, as in most men, an indurated, heterogeneous fabric of many dates, and of no settled character, in which the man is imprisoned. Then there can be enlargement, and the man of to-day scarcely recognizes the man of yesterday. And such should be the outward biography of man in time, a putting off of dead circumstances day by day, as he renews his raiment day by day. But to us, in our lapsed estate, resting, not advancing, resisting, not cooperating with the divine expansion, this growth comes by shocks.

We cannot part with our friend. We cannot let our angels go. We do not believe in the riches of the soul, in its proper eternity and omnipresence. We do not believe there is any force in to-day to rival or recreate that beautiful yesterday. We linger in the ruins of the old tent, where once we had bread and shelter and organs, nor believe that the spirit can feed, cover, and nerve us again. We cannot again find aught so dear, so sweet, so graceful. But we sit and weep in vain. The voice of the Almighty saith, "Up and onward forevermore!" We cannot stay amid the ruins. Neither will we rely on the new; and so we walk ever with reverted eyes, like those monsters who look backwards.

And yet the compensations of calamity are made apparent to the understanding also, after long intervals of time. A fever, a mutilation, a cruel disappointment, a loss of wealth, a loss of friends, seems at the moment unpaid loss, and unpayable. But the sure years reveal the deep remedial force that underlies all facts. The death of a dear friend, wife, brother, lover, which seemed nothing but privation, somewhat later assumes the aspect of a guide or genius; for it commonly operates revolutions in our way of life, terminates an epoch of infancy or of youth which was waiting to be closed, breaks up a wanted occupation, or a household, or style of living, and allows the formation of new ones more friendly to the growth of character. It permits or constrains the formation of new acquaintances, and the reception of new influences that prove of the first importance to the next years; and the man or woman who would have remained a sunny garden flower, with no room for its roots and too much sunshine for its head, by the falling of the walls and the neglect of the gardener, is made the banyan of the forest, yielding shade and fruit to wide neighborhoods of men.

This world would be a delightful place to live in. However, Man's worst enemy is always man. They really cause all the trouble. The greater part of the pain, sorrow and misery in life is purely a human invention, yet man, with cowardly irreverence, dares to throws the blames on mother nature. It comes through breaking laws, laws natural, physical, civic, mental or moral. These are laws which man knows, but he disregards; he takes chances; he thinks he can dodge results in some way. But nature says, "He who breaks, pays."

That which can be prevented, should be prevented. It all rests with the individual. The "preventable" exists in three degrees: First, that which is due to the individual solely and directly; second, that which he suffers through the wrongdoing of those around him, other individuals; third, those instances wherein he is the unnecessary victim of the wrongs of society, the innocent legatee of the folly of humanity and society is but the massing of millions of individuals with the heritage of manners, customs and laws they have received from the past.

We sometimes feel heart-sick and weary in facing failure, when the fortune that seemed almost in our fingers slips away because of the envy, malice or treachery of someone else. We bow under the weight of a sorrow that makes all life grow dark and the star of hope fade from our vision; or we meet some unnecessary misfortune with a dumb, helpless despair. "It is all wrong," we say, "it is cruel, it is unjust. Why is it permitted?" And, in the very intensity of our feeling, we half-unconsciously repeat the words over and over again, in monotonous iteration, as if in some way the very repetition might bring relief, might somehow soothe us. Yet, in most instances, it could be prevented. No suffering is caused in the world by right. Whatever sorrow there is that is preventable, comes from in harmony or wrong of some kind.

For example. When a terrible fire makes a city desolate and a nation mourn, the investigation that follows usually shows that a little human foresight could have prevented it, or at least, lessened the horror of it all. If chemicals or dynamite are stored in any building in excess of what wise legislation declares is safe, someone has been cruelly careless. Perhaps it is some inspector who has been disloyal to his trust, by permitting bribes to chloroform his sense of duty. If the lack of fire-escapes adds its quota to the list of deaths, or if the avarice of the owner has made his building a fire-trap, public feeling becomes intense, the newspapers are justly loud in their protests, and in demands that the guilty ones be punished. "If the laws already on the statute books do not cover the situation," we hear from day to day, "new laws will be framed to make a repetition of the tragedy impossible"; we are promised all kinds of reforms; the air seems filled with a spirit of regeneration; the mercury of public indignation rises to the point where "fever-heat" seems a mild, inadequate term.

Then, as the horror begins to fade in the perspective of the past, men go quietly back to their own personal cares and duties, and the mighty wave of righteous protest that threatened so much, dies in gentle lapping on the shore. What has been all men concern seems soon to concern no one. The tremendous energy of the authorities seems like the gesture of a drunken man, that starts from his shoulder with a force that would almost fell an ox but when it reaches the hand it has expended itself, and the hand drops listlessly in the air with hardly power enough to disturb the serenity of a butterfly. There is always a little progress, a slight advance, and it is only the constant accumulation of these steps that is giving to the world greater dominion over the preventable.

Poverty has no necessary place in life. It is a disease that results from the weakness, sin, and selfishness of humanity. Nature is boundless in her generosity; the world produces sufficient to give food, clothing, and comfort to every individual. Poverty is preventable. Poverty may result from the shiftlessness, idleness, intemperance, improvidence, lack of purpose or evil-doing of the individual himself.

If the causes do not exist in the individual, they may be found in the second class, in the wrongdoing of those around him, in the oppression of labor by capital, in the grinding process by which corporations seek to crush the individual. The individual may be the victim of any of a thousand phases of the wrong of others. The poverty caused by the third class, the weakness and injustice of human laws and human institutions, is also preventable, but to reach the cause requires time and united heroic effort of all individuals.

It is ever the little things that make up the sum of human misery. All the wild animals of the world combined do but trifling damage, when compared with the ravages of insect pests. The crimes of humanity, the sins that make us start back frightened, do not cause as much sorrow and unhappiness in life as the multitude of little sins, of omission and commission, that the individual, and millions like him, must meet every day.

The world is learning the great truth, that the best way to prevent crime is to study the sociological conditions in which it flourishes, to seek to give each man a better chance of living his real life by removing, if possible, the elements that make wrong easy, and to him, almost necessary, and by inspiring him to fight life's battle bravely with all the help others can give him.

PERCEPTIONS AND PROPOSITIONS

Every one will readily allow, that there is a considerable difference between the perceptions of the mind. We may observe a like distinction to run through all the other perceptions of the mind. A man in a fit of anger, is actuated in a very different manner from one who only thinks of that emotion. If you tell me, that any person is in love, I easily understand your meaning, and form a just conception of his situation; but never can mistake that conception for the real disorders and agitations of the passion. When we reflect on our past sentiments and affections, our thought is a faithful mirror, and copies its objects truly; but the colors which it employs are faint and dull, in comparison of those in which our original perceptions were clothed. It requires no nice discernment or metaphysical head to mark the distinction between them.

Nothing, at first view, may seem more unbounded than the thought of man, which not only escapes human power and authority, but is not even restrained within the limits of nature and reality. But though our thought seems to possess this unbounded liberty, we shall find, upon a nearer examination, that it is really confined within very narrow limits, and that all this creative power of the mind amounts to no more than the faculty of compounding, transposing, augmenting, or diminishing the materials afforded us by the senses and experience.

The objects of human reason or inquiry may naturally be divided into two kinds, Relations of Ideas, and Matters of Fact. Reasoning's concerning matter of fact seem to be founded on the relation of cause and effect. By means of that relation alone we can go beyond the evidence of our memory and senses. If you were to ask a man, why he believes any matter of fact, which is absent; for instance,. A man finding a watch or any other machine in a desert island he would give you a reason; and this reason would be some other fact; he would conclude that there had once been men in that island. All our reasoning's concerning fact are of the same nature. And here it is constantly supposed that there is a connexion between the present fact and that which is inferred from it. Were there nothing to bind them together, the inference would be entirely precarious. The hearing of an articulate voice and rational discourse in the dark assures us of the presence of some person: Why? because these are the effects of the human make and fabric, and closely connected with it. If we anatomize all the other reasoning's of this nature, we shall find that they are founded on the relation of cause and effect, and that this relation is either near or remote, direct or collateral. Heat and light are collateral effects of fire, and the one effect may justly be inferred from the other.

If we would satisfy ourselves, therefore, concerning the nature of that evidence, which assures us of matters of fact, we must inquire how we arrive at the knowledge of cause and effect. Proposition, that causes and effects are discover-able, not by reason but by experience, will readily be admitted with regard to such objects, as we remember to have once been altogether unknown to us; since we must be conscious of the utter inability, which we then lay under, of foretelling what would arise from them. In short, every effect is a distinct event from its cause.

It is confessed, that the utmost effort of human reason is to reduce the principles, productive of natural phenomena, to a greater simplicity, and to resolve the many particular effects into a few general causes, by means of reasoning's from analogy, experience, and observation. But as to the causes of these general causes, we should in vain attempt their discovery; nor shall we ever be able to satisfy ourselves, by any particular explication of them. These ultimate springs and principles are totally shut up from human curiosity and inquiry. Elasticity, gravity, cohesion of parts, communication of motion by impulse; these are probably the ultimate causes and principles which we shall ever discover in nature; and we may esteem ourselves sufficiently happy, if, by accurate inquiry and reasoning, we can trace up the particular phenomena to, or near to, these general principles.

Humans have not yet attained any tolerable satisfaction with regard to the questions we proposed. Each solution still gives rise to a new question as difficult as the foregoing, and leads us on to further inquiries. When it is asked, What is the nature of all our reasoning's concerning matter of fact? the proper answer seems to be, that they are founded on the relation of cause and effect. When again it is asked, What is the foundation of all our reasoning's and conclusions concerning that relation? it may be replied in one word, Experience. But if we still carry on our sifting humor, and ask, What is the foundation of all conclusions from experience? This implies a new question, which may be of more difficult solution and explication. Great thinkers that give themselves airs of superior wisdom and sufficiency, have a hard task when they encounter persons of inquisitive dispositions, who push them from every corner to which they retreat, and who are sure at last to bring them to some dangerous dilemma. The best expedient to prevent this confusion, is to be modest in our pretensions; and even to discover the difficulty ourselves before it is objected to us. By this means, we may make a kind of merit of our very ignorance.

Nature has kept us at a great distance from most of her secrets, and has afforded us only the knowledge of a few superficial qualities of objects; while she conceals from us those powers and principles on which the influence of those objects entirely depends. Our senses inform us of the color, weight, and consistency of bread; but neither sense nor reason can ever inform us of those qualities which fit it for the nourishment and support of a human body. Sight or feeling conveys an idea of the actual motion of bodies; but as to that wonderful force or power, which would carry on a moving body for ever in a continued change of place, and which bodies never lose but by communicating it to others; of this we cannot form the most distant conception. But notwithstanding this ignorance of natural powers and principles, we always presume, when we see like sensible qualities, that they have like secret powers, and expect that effects, similar to those which we have experienced, will follow from them.

All reasoning's may be divided into two kinds, namely, demonstrative reasoning, or that concerning relations of ideas, and moral reasoning, or that concerning matter of fact and existence. That there are no demonstrative arguments in the case seems evident; since it implies no contradiction that the course of nature may change, and that an object, seemingly like those which we have experienced, may be attended with different or contrary effects.

If we, therefore, engaged by arguments to put trust in past experience, and make it the standard of our future judgment, these arguments must be probable only, or such as regard matter of fact and real existence. We have said that all arguments concerning existence are founded on the relation of cause and effect; that our knowledge of that relation is derived entirely from experience; and that all our experimental conclusions proceed upon the supposition that the future will be conformable to the past. To endeavor, therefore, the proof of this last supposition by probable arguments, or arguments regarding existence, must be evidently going in a circle, and taking that for granted, which is the very point in question.

In reality, our arguments from experiences are founded on the similarity which we discover among natural objects, and by which we are induced to expect effects similar to those which we have found to follow from such objects. And though the arrogant will ever pretend to dispute the authority of experience, or to reject that great guide of human life, it may surely be allowed a person to have so much curiosity at least as to examine the principle of human nature, which gives this mighty authority to experience, and makes us draw advantage from that similarity which nature has placed among different objects. From causes which appear similar we expect similar effects. This is the sum of all our experimental conclusions. Now it seems evident that, if this conclusion were formed by reason, it would be as perfect at first, and upon one instance, as after ever so long a course of experience. It is only after a long course of uniform experiments in any kind, that we attain a firm reliance and security with regard to a particular event. Now where is that process of reasoning which, from one instance, draws a conclusion, so different from that which it infers from a hundred instances that are nowise different from that another?

We say that the one proposition is an inference from the other. But we can confess that the inference is not intuitive; neither is it demonstrative: Of what nature is it, then? To say it is experimental, is begging the question. For all inferences from experience suppose, as their foundation, that the future will resemble the past, and that similar powers will be conjoined with similar sensible qualities. If there be any suspicion that the course of nature may change, and that the past may be no rule for the future, all experience becomes useless, and can give rise to no inference or conclusion. It is impossible, therefore, that any arguments from experience can prove this resemblance of the past to the future; since all these arguments are founded on the supposition of that resemblance. Let the course of things be allowed hitherto ever so regular; that alone, without some new argument or inference, proves not that, for the future, it will continue so. In vain do you pretend to have learned the nature of bodies from your past experience. Their secret nature, and consequently all their effects and influence, may change, without any change in their sensible qualities.

There may be no reason to infer the existence of one from the appearance of the other. And in a word, such a person, without more experience, could never employ his conjecture or reasoning concerning any matter of fact, or be assured of anything beyond what was immediately present to his memory and senses.

Suppose, again, that he has acquired more experience, and has lived so long in the world as to have observed familiar objects or events to be constantly conjoined together; what is the consequence of this experience? He immediately infers the existence of one object from the appearance of the other. Yet he has not, by all his experience, acquired any idea or knowledge of the secret power by which the one object produces the other; nor is it, by any process of reasoning, he is engaged to draw this inference. But still he finds himself determined to draw it: And though he should be convinced that his understanding has no part in the operation, he would nevertheless continue in the same course of thinking. There is some other principle which determines him to form such a conclusion.

This principle is custom or habit. For wherever the repetition of any particular act or operation produces a propensity to renew the same act or operation, without being impelled by any reasoning or process of the understanding, we always say, that this propensity is the effect of custom. By employing that word, we pretend not to have given the ultimate reason of such a propensity. We only point out a principle of human nature, which is universally acknowledged, and which is well known by its effects. Perhaps we can push our inquiries no farther, or pretend to give the cause of this cause; but must rest contented with it as the ultimate principle, which we can assign, of all our conclusions from experience.It is sufficient satisfaction, that we can go so far, without repining at the narrowness of our faculties because they will carry us no farther. And it is certain we here advance a very intelligible proposition at least, if not a true one, when we assert that, after the constant conjunction of two objects-heat and flame, for instance, weight and solidity, we are determined by custom alone to expect the one from the appearance of the other. This hypothesis seems even the only one which explains the difficulty, why we draw, from a thousand instances, an inference which we are not able to draw from one instance, that is, in no respect, different from them. Reason is incapable of any such variation. The conclusions which it draws from considering one circle are the same which it would form upon surveying all the circles in the universe. But no man, having seen only one body move after being impelled by another, could infer that every other body will move after a like impulse. All inferences from experience, therefore, are effects of custom, not of reasoning.

Custom, then, is the great guide of human life. It is that principle alone which renders our experience useful to us, and makes us expect, for the future, a similar train of events with those which have appeared in the past.

Without the influence of custom, we should be entirely ignorant of every matter of fact beyond what is immediately present to the memory and senses. We should never know how to adjust means to ends, or to employ our natural powers in the production of any effect. There would be an end at once of all action, as well as of the chief part of speculation.

But here it may be proper to remark, that though our conclusions from experience carry us beyond our memory and senses, and assure us of matters of fact which happened in the most distant places and most remote ages, yet some fact must always be present to the senses or memory, from which we may first proceed in drawing these conclusions.

In a word, if we proceed not upon some fact, present to the memory or senses, our reasoning's would be merely hypothetical; and however the particular links might be connected with each other, the whole chain of inferences would have nothing to support it, nor could we ever, by its means, arrive at the knowledge of any real existence.

What then, is the conclusion of the matter? A simple one: Believes of matter of fact or real existence is derived merely from some object, present to the memory or senses, and a customary conjunction between that and some other object. Or in other words; having found, in many instances, that any two kinds of objects, flame and heat, snow and cold, have always been conjoined together; if flame or snow be presented anew to the senses, the mind is carried by custom to expect heat or cold, and to believe that such a quality does exist, and will discover itself upon a nearer approach. This belief is the necessary result of placing the mind in such circumstances. It is an operation of the soul, when we are so situated, as unavoidable as to feel the passion of love, when we receive benefits; or hatred, when we meet with injuries. All these operations are a species of natural instincts, which no reasoning or process of the thought and understanding is able either to produce or to prevent.

Nothing is more free than the imagination of man; and though it cannot exceed that original stock of ideas furnished by the internal and external senses, it has unlimited power of mixing, compounding, separating, and dividing these ideas, in all the varieties of fiction and vision. It can feign a train of events, with all the appearance of reality, ascribe to them a particular time and place, conceive them as existent, and paint them out to itself with every circumstance, that belongs to any historical fact, which it believes with the greatest certainty. Wherein, therefore, consists the difference between such a fiction and belief? It lies not merely in any peculiar idea, which is annexed to such a conception as commands our assent, and which is wanting to every known fiction. For as the mind has authority over all its ideas, it could voluntarily annex this particular idea to any fiction, and consequently be able to believe whatever it pleases; contrary to what we find by daily experience. We can, in our conception, join the head of a man to the body of a horse; but it is not in our power to believe that such an animal has ever really existed.

It follows, therefore, that the difference between fiction and belief lies in some sentiment or feeling, which is annexed to the latter, not to the former, and which depends not on the will, nor can be commanded at pleasure. It must be excited by nature, like all other sentiments; and must arise from the particular situation, in which the mind is placed at any particular juncture. Whenever any object is presented to the memory or senses, it immediately, by the force of custom, carries the imagination to conceive that object, which is usually conjoined to it; and this conception is attended with a feeling or sentiment, different from the loose reveries of the fancy. In this consists the whole nature of belief. For as there is no matter of fact which we believe so firmly that we cannot conceive the contrary, there would be no difference between the conception assented to and that which is rejected, were it not for some sentiment which distinguishes the one from the other. If you see a billiard-ball moving towards another, on a smooth table, you can easily conceive it to stop upon contact. This conception implies no contradiction; but still it feels very differently from that conception by which I represent to myself the impulse and the communication of motion from one ball to another.

Were we to attempt a definition of this sentiment, we should, perhaps, find it a very difficult, if not an impossible task; in the same manner as if we should endeavor to define the feeling of cold or passion of anger, to a creature who never had any experience of these sentiments. Belief is the true and proper name of this feeling; and no one is ever at a loss to know the meaning of that term; because every man is every moment conscious of the sentiment represented by it. It may not, however, be improper to attempt a description of this sentiment; in hopes we may, by that means, arrive at some analogies, which may afford a more perfect explication of it. I say, then, that belief is nothing but a more vivid, lively, forcible, firm, steady conception of an object, than what the imagination alone is ever able to attain.

These variety of terms, is intended only to express that act of the mind, which renders realities, or what is taken for such, more present to us than fictions, causes them to weigh more in the thought, and gives them a superior influence on the passions and imagination. Provided we agree about the thing, it is needless to dispute about the terms. The imagination has the command over all its ideas, and can join and mix and vary them, in all the ways possible. It may conceive fictitious objects with all the circumstances of place and time. It may set them, in a manner, before our eyes, in their true colors, just as they might have existed. But as it is impossible that this faculty of imagination can ever, of itself, reach belief, it is evident that belief consists not in the peculiar nature or order of ideas, but in the manner of their conception, and in their feeling to the mind.

Our ignorance of the real cause of any event has the same influence on the understanding, and begets a like species of belief or opinion.

There is certainly a probability, which arises from a superiority of chances on any side; and according as this superiority increases, and surpasses the opposite chances, the probability receives a proportionate increase, and begets still a higher degree of belief or assent to that side, in which we discover the superiority. If a dye were marked with one figure or number of spots on four sides, and with another figure or number of spots on the two remaining sides, it would be more probable, that the former would turn up than the latter; though, if it had a thousand sides marked in the same manner, and only one side different, the probability would be much higher, and our belief or expectation of the event more steady and secure. This process of the thought or reasoning may seem trivial and obvious; but to those who consider it more narrowly, it may, perhaps, afford matter for curious speculation.

FRIENDSHIPS AND SOCIALIZATION

We have a great deal more kindness than is ever spoken. Barring all the selfishness that chills like east winds the world, the whole human family is bathed with an element of love like a fine ether. How many persons we meet in houses, whom we scarcely speak to, whom yet we honor, and who honor us! How many we see in the street, or sit with in church, whom, though silently, we warmly rejoice to be with! From the highest degree of passionate love, to the lowest degree of goodwill, they make the sweetness of life.

Our intellectual and active powers increase with our affection. The scholar sits down to write, and all his years of meditation do not furnish him with one good thought or happy expression; but it is necessary to write a letter to a friend, an forthwith, troops of gentle thoughts invest themselves, on every hand, with chosen words. See in any house where virtue and self-respect abide, the palpitation which the approach of a stranger causes. A commended stranger is expected and announced, and an uneasiness between pleasure and pain invades all the hearts of a household. His arrival almost brings fear to the good hearts that would welcome him. The house is dusted, all things fly into their places, the old coat is exchanged for the new, and they must get up a dinner if they can. Of a commended stranger, only the good report is told by others, only the good and new is heard by us. He stands to us for humanity. He is, what we wish. Having imagined and invested him, we ask how we should stand related in conversation and action with such a man, and are uneasy with fear. The same idea exalts conversation with him. We talk better than we are wont. We have the nimblest fancy, a richer memory, and our dumb devil has taken leave for the time. For long hours we can continue a series of sincere, graceful, rich communications, drawn from the oldest, secretes experience, so that they who sit by, of our own kinsfolk and acquaintance, shall feel a lively surprise at our unusual powers. But as soon as the stranger begins to intrude his partialities, his definitions, his defects, into the conversation, it is all over. He has heard the first, the last and best, he will ever hear from us. He is no stranger now. Vulgarity, ignorance, misapprehension, are old acquaintances. Now, when he comes, he may get the order, the dress, and the dinner, but the throbbing of the heart, and the communications of the soul, no more.

What is so delicious as a just and firm encounter of two, in a thought, in a feeling? How beautiful, on their approach to this beating heart, the steps and forms of the gifted and the true! The moment we indulge our affections, the earth is metamorphosed; there is no winter, and no night; all tragedies, all ennui's vanish; all duties even; nothing fills the proceeding eternity but the forms all radiant of beloved persons. Let the soul be assured that somewhere in the universe it should rejoin its friend, and it would be content and cheerful alone for many years.

The other element of friendship is tenderness. We are Holden to men by every sort of tie, by blood, by pride, by fear, by hope, by lucre, by lust, by hate, by admiration, by every circumstance and badge and trifle, but we can scarce believe that so much character can subsist in another as to draw us by love. Can another be so blessed, and we so pure, that we can offer him tenderness? When a man becomes dear to me, I have touched the goal of fortune.

Friendship may be said to require natures so rare and costly, each so well-tempered, and so happily adapted. Friendship requires that rare mean between likeness and unlikeness, that piques each with the presence of power and of consent in the other party. Are you the friend of your friend's buttons, or of his thought? To a great heart he will still be a stranger in a thousand particulars, that he may come near in the holiest ground. Leave it to girls and boys to regard a friend as property, and to suck a short and all-confounding pleasure instead of the noblest benefits.

One is thrown in life with a great many people who, though not actively bad, though they may not willfully lead us astray, yet take no pains with themselves, neglect their own minds, and direct the conversation to petty puerility or mere gossip; who do not seem to realize that conversation may by a little effort be made most instructive and delightful, without being in any way pedantic; or, on the other hand, may be allowed to drift into a mere morass of muddy thought and weedy words. There is hardly anyone from whom we may not learn much, if only they will trouble themselves to tell us. Nay, even if they teach us nothing, they may help us by the stimulus of intelligent questions, or the warmth of sympathy. But if they do neither, then indeed their companionship, if companionship it can be called, is mere waste of time.

Much certainly of the happiness and purity of our lives depends on our making a wise choice of our companions and friends. If our friends are badly chosen they will inevitably drag us down; if well they will raise us up. Yet many people seem to trust in this matter to the chapter of accident. It is well and right, indeed, to be courteous and considerate to every one with whom we are brought into contact, but to choose them as real friends is another matter. Some seem to make a man a friend, or try to do so, because he lives near, because he is in the same business, travels on the same line of railway, or for some other trivial reason. There cannot be a greater mistake.

Let us buy our entrance to this guild by a long probation. Why should we desecrate noble and beautiful souls by intruding on them? Why insist on rash personal relations with your friend? Why go to his house, or know his mother and brother and sisters? Why be visited by him at your own? Are these things material to our covenant? Leave this touching and clawing. Let him be to me a spirit. A message, a thought, a sincerity, a glance from him I want, but not news, nor pottage. I can get politics, and chat, and neighborly conveniences, from cheaper companions. Should not the society of my friend be to me poetic, pure, universal, and great as nature itself? Ought I to feel that our tie is profane in comparison with yonder bar of cloud that sleeps on the horizon, or that clump of waving grass that divides the brook? Let us not vilify but raise it to that standard. That great defying eye, that scornful beauty of his mien and action, do not pique yourself on reducing, but rather fortify and enhance. Worship his superiorities; wish him not less by a thought, but hoard and tell them all. Guard him as thy counterpart. Let him be to thee forever a sort of beautiful enemy, untamable, devoutly revered, and not a trivial convenient to be soon outgrown and cast aside.

No doubt, much as worthy friends add to the happiness and value of life, we must in the main depend on ourselves, and every one is his own best friend or worst enemy. Some people never seem to appreciate their friends till they have lost them. If, then, we choose our friends for what they are, not for what they have, and if we deserve so great a blessing, then they will be always with us, preserved even in absence.

LIFE VALUES

Life is earnest! is a very old lesson, and we are never too old to learn it. 'Life is an art'. Life seems to be a marvel the older we grow! So far from becoming more intelligible, it becomes a greater wonder every day. However, we must toil on and do what every day brings us, and do it as well as we can, and better, if possible, than anybody else.

The things that annoy us in life are after all very trifling things, if we always bear in mind for what purpose we are here. It is true we cannot understand it, but we can understand that, one can enjoys his life as long as it lasts.

Life may grow more strange and awful each day, but the more strange and awful it grows, the more it reveals to us its truest meaning and reality, and the deepest depth of its of these challenges, behold it was very good. Enjoy the precious years that are added to your life, with constant gratitude, with quiet and purity of soul in the small, or even the large cares of life.

Yes, every day adds a new thin layer of new thoughts, and these layers form the texture of our character. The materials come floating towards us, but the way in which they settle down depends much on the ebb and flow within us. We can do much to keep off foreign elements, and to attach and retain those which serve best in building up a strong rock. But from time to time a great sorrow breaks through all the strata of our soul all is up-heaved, shattered, distorted. In nature all that is grand dates from such convulsions why should we wish for a new smooth surface, or let our sorrows be covered by the flat sediment of everyday life?

If we feel that this life can only be a link in a chain without beginning and without end, in a circle which has its beginning and its end everywhere and nowhere, we learn to bear it, and to enjoy it too, in a new sense. What we achieve here assumes a new.

I suppose that most of us, sooner or later in life, have felt how the whole world this horrible world, as we call it is changed as if by magic, if once we can make up our mind to give men credit for good motives, never to be suspicious, never to think evil, never to think ourselves better than our neighbors. Trust a man to be true and good, and, even if he is not, your trust will tend to make him true and good.

Sorrow is necessary and good for men; one learns to understand that each joy must be indemnified by suffering, that each new tie which knits our hearts to this life must be loosed again, and the tighter and the closer it was knit, the keener the pain of loosening it. Should we then attach our hearts to nothing, and pass quietly and unsympathetically through this world, as if we had nothing to do with it? We neither could nor ought to act so. Nature itself knits the first tie between parents and children, and new ties through our whole life. We are not here for reward, for the enjoyment of undisturbed peace or from mere accident, but for trial, for improvement, perhaps for punishment; for the only union which can secure the happiness of men.

We have toiled for many years and been troubled with many questionings, but what is the end of it all? We must learn to become simple again like little children. That is all we have a right to be: for this life was meant to be the childhood of our souls, and the more we try to be what we were meant to be, the better for us. Let us use the powers of our minds with the greatest freedom and love of truth, but let us never forget that we are, as Newton said, like children playing on the seashore, while the great ocean of truth lies undiscovered before us.

Think only what it was to believe in an order of the world, though it be no more at first than a belief that the sun will never overstep his bounds. It was all the difference between a chaos and a cosmos, between the blind play of chance and an intelligible and therefore an intelligent providence. How many souls, even now when everything else has failed them, when they have parted with the most cherished convictions of their childhood, when their faith in man has been poisoned, and when the apparent triumph of all that is selfish, ignoble, and hideous has made them throw up the cause of truth, of righteousness, and innocence as no longer worth fighting for, at least in this world; how many, I say, have found their last peace and comfort in the contemplation of the order of the world, whether manifested in the unvarying movement of the stars, or revealed in the unvarying number of the petals and stamens and pistils of the smallest forget-me-not. How many have felt that to belong to this cosmos, to this beautiful order of nature, is something at least to rest on, something to trust, something to believe, when everything else has failed. To us, this perception of law and order in the world may seem very little, but to the ancient dwellers on earth, who had little else to support them, it was everything because, if once perceived, if once understood, it could never be taken from them.

We can and learn to see a meaning in everything. No doubt we cannot always see cause and effect, and it is well we cannot. It is quite true that we do not always get our deserts. And yet we must believe that we do—only if we knew it, the whole fabric of the world would be destroyed, there would be neither virtue nor vice in the whole world, nothing but calculation. We should avoid the rails laid down by the world because we should know that the engine would be sure to come and mangle us. In this way the world holds together, and it could not in any other way.

There is to a beauty and mystery and sanctity about flowers, and when I see them come and go, no one knows whence and whither, I ask what more miracles do we want, what better, more beautiful, more orderly world could we wish to belong to than that by which we are surrounded and supported on all sides? Where is there a flaw or a fault? Then why should we fear unless the flaws are within us, and we will not see the blessing and the rest which we might enjoy if we only trusted to the author of all that beauty, order, and wisdom about us. It is a perfect sin not to be happy in this world, and how much of the misery which there is, is the work of men, or could be removed by men, if they would but work together for each others' good.

IDEAL AND BASIS

Artistic creation and appreciation brings another characteristic unfolding of life; and this also demonstrates an inner relation of man to the world, and can be developed only when this relation is acknowledged. In the first place, for this creation and appreciation a deliverance of life from the turmoil of ends and interests, which at first sway our existence, is essential; artistic creation and appreciation involves a resting and a tarrying in itself. If the world were no more than this turmoil, if it did not in some way attain to self-consciousness, how could such a deliverance be brought about? If a self-conscious life were not present in man, how could a longing for an artistic moulding of life arise in him? But an arousing of an inner life in things, the revelation of a soul, is accomplished not through imparting something from without, but through a meeting together of things and human endeavour. On the other hand, the spiritual expresses itself in a visible form and in doing so mould itself. The chief thing in this connection is not mere beauty, a preparation for idle enjoyment, but a truth, a revelation of contents, a further development of life through and above the antithesis. How could something invisible and something visible, to express the matter briefly, find a common ground and combine together in a common action if nature were not more than the mere web of relations into which the mechanistic conception of it transforms it; if spiritual life were not more than the subjective form of life that it is supposed to be, according to general opinion; if from that form of life an inner life did not arise, and beyond all subjectivity attain to a full activity, and thus to the building up of a reality within its own province? That we do not simply become aware of a movement within ourselves, and then read it into nature, but only take up and lead to its own truth that which strives upward in nature, is again testified by the inner advance of this striving through its contact with the world, and by the infinite abundance of particular contents which are revealed to us in the world and which continually aid in our development.

Again, our life experiences the most important elevation in that it takes up and carries further a movement of the whole, and is liberated from the narrowness of the particular sphere, without merging into a vague infinity. To realize clearly that we belong to the world, and energetically to amplify this relation, is of the greatest significance for artistic creation and appreciation. For it is only by becoming firmly established in these relations that artistic endeavour is able to resist the tendency to degenerate into play and pleasure a tendency which threatens it with inner destruction; as in a similar manner the work of thought must guard itself from degenerating into mere reflection. In the realms of thought and art there remains much that is alien, ever surmise and symbol; but even symbol is not to be disdained, if it serves an important truth.

Accordingly, life-developments of various and related kinds arise: with their manifold experiences they strive to attain to a harmony and a union with one another. They can seek these only on the basis of a self-consciousness of reality; find them only through their unification in a universal life, to which each individual tendency leads. Representations of the whole are attempted at the highest points of creative activity by philosophy, religion, and art; these representations accompany, indeed govern, the work in these spheres of life through history. But the limitations of our capacity, through which we are unable to give a suitable form to necessary contents, and through which we attribute and must attribute human traits to that which should lead us beyond the human, are of particular force in this matter of forming a representation of the whole; and, indeed, this is the more so the further we remove ourselves from that which may be immediately transformed in work.

These representations of the whole are, therefore, inadequate; their content of truth is clothed in a wrapping of myth, and humanity lies under the danger of taking the myth for the chief thing and thus of obscuring the truth, and this must produce an incalculable amount of error and strife. Still, it is impossible to give up all claim to these representations of the whole; for they alone make the fact of our belonging to the whole and of the presence of the whole in our life quite clear and enable it to exert a far-reaching influence. Only with their help can the degeneration of life to the intolerable insignificance of the narrowly human be resisted; only with their help can a movement from whole to whole begin.

It is a leading idea of our whole investigation that only from the life-process itself are we able to orientate ourselves in relation to ourselves and the world; and this idea is in agreement with the present mode of thought in science. But to apply to our own time that which is already acknowledged in general ideas is by no means simple. To give the life-process such a position in our thought and to estimate it so highly is possible only when life is distinctly distinguished from the states of the mere subject, from the mere reflex of the environment in the individual. This detachment cannot be accomplished unless we comprehend as a whole that which exists in individual manifestations of life; distinguish different levels in life, indicate relations and movements within them, and thus advance to new experiences of life; reveal a union of fact, a distinctive synthesis in life, which from a transcendent unity shapes the multiplicity that it contains.

A REVELATION

I have a dream, that happy days and nights are coming and it will feel so amazing. People who were once your enemies will become your friends, smiles on lovely faces will be beaming. At a certain point suffering will end there will be days and nights of sweet stimulation.

The place to be happy is here, and the way to be happy is to make others happy. These ways of sharing happiness will give us good long days. There will be so much joys in our eyes, no tears or fears.

There will be peace between the superpowers in the north, south, east, and west. There will be a long peace which will ultimately give us joy and happiness. Humans will no longer need to indulge in bodily pleasures to attain a good a fulfilling life. A life that has meaning always feels purposeful and significant.

Each human will then know his worth, and keep things under his feet. Humans will no longer peep or steal, or skulk up and down with the air of a charity-boy, a bastard, or an interloper, in the world which exists for him. The sculpture in the memory of beings is going to be filled with established harmony.

We will no longer have a lack of motivation, has a side effect of our lives, which would normally leave us feeling deflated and empty handed. Yes, it will be possible to breath joy and happiness back in our lives, by actively seeking out various sources of inspiration in the world. We will be able to illuminate truths, amplify unheard or overlooked voices, alter our lives, change negative to positive perspectives. Our lives will also be educated, activate, inspire, helps clarify and aspire the uniqueness in us, to take several concrete steps and changes to help each other with a neighborly love.

Mark my words you will stay inspired and fend off the ruts of being unproductive and connecting with beauty in life. This fulfilling life you've always dream of is going to come true.

Life is a journey, and the path which was once not so clear, each moment in our lives will blooms not just with wonders and possibilities. The path we've traversed will lead us to the desired destination

It will be the sweetest life we will ever know for each day, and each night the world will feel just right. I may not live to see it, but you will.

ABOUT THE AUTHOR

Wayne Lindsey is a Consultant Psychological Therapist, and a Licensed Mindfulness teacher

Most of his writings are centered around self-healing, Positive personal development, Mindfulness, Existential philosophy, Adler (Individual psychology).

In his leisure time Lindsey enjoys Go-karting, singing at weddings, gigs, and other party functions.

He is the author of several other books and several articles including: *The Love-Response® Helper* and *Assisting A Life*.